Edward D. Andrews

The MACCABEES

The Hasmonaeans Dynasty between Malachi and Matthew

THE MACCABEES

The Hasmonaean Dynasty between Malachi and Matthew

Edward D. Andrews

Christian Publishing House

Cambridge, Ohio

Unless otherwise stated, Scripture quotations are from Updated American Standard Version (UASV) Copyright © 2022 by Christian Publishing House

THE MACCABEES: The Hasmonaean Dynasty between Malachi and Matthew by Edward D. Andrews

ISBN-13: **9798374762365**

Table of Contents

Preface

The Maccabees: The Hasmonaeans Dynasty between Malachi and Matthew is a comprehensive study of the Hasmonaeans dynasty and its role in shaping the history of ancient Judaism. The book delves into the political, religious and social aspects of the Hasmonaeans and how they influenced the emergence of the Pharisees and the Sadducees, two influential groups that appear in the Gospel accounts as well as in the writings of first-century Jewish historian Josephus.

The Hasmonaeans came to power at a time when many Jews were succumbing to the appeal of Hellenism, or Greek culture and philosophy. The tension between Hellenism and Judaism peaked when the Seleucid rulers defiled the temple in Jerusalem, dedicating it to Zeus. A dynamic Jewish leader, Judah Maccabee, of a family known as the Hasmonaeans, led a rebel army that freed the temple from Greek hands.

The book also examines the expansion and oppression of the Hasmonaeans, who, after achieving their religious goal of restoring worship at Jehovah's temple, turned to politics, resulting in many Jews leaving them. The Hasmonaeans continued their fight against the Seleucid rulers, formed a treaty with Rome, and sought to establish an independent Jewish State. However, their rule came to an end when their son-in-law, Ptolemy, assassinated Simon, the leader of the Hasmonaeans, along with two of his sons while they were banqueting near Jericho.

The book also explores the emergence of the Pharisees and the Sadducees, two sects that developed as a result of the Hasmonaean's political and religious ideologies. The Pharisees and Sadducees both emerged during the time of John Hyrcanus reign, and their rise was closely tied to the political and religious developments of the time. Hyrcanus initially supported the Pharisees, but their relationship broke down, leading him to outlaw their religious ordinances and align himself with the Sadducees.

The book also examines the final years of the Hasmonaean kingdom under the reign of Alexander Jannaeus, who ruled from 103-

76 BC. Alexander Jannaeus broke with previous policy and freely declared himself both high priest and king. The conflicts between the Hasmonaeans and the Pharisees intensified, even leading to a civil war in which 50,000 Jews perished.

The Maccabees: The Hasmonaeans Dynasty between Malachi and Matthew is an invaluable resource for scholars, students and anyone interested in understanding the complex history of ancient Judaism and its impact on the formation of religious sects and the emergence of key figures in the New Testament.

Introduction

The Maccabees: The Hasmonaeans Dynasty between Malachi and Matthew is a comprehensive study of the Hasmonaeans dynasty and its impact on the history of ancient Judaism. The Hasmonaeans, a family of priests and warriors, came to power in the 2nd century BC during a time of great turmoil and change in the Jewish world. They led a successful rebellion against the Seleucid Empire, which had sought to impose Greek culture and religion on the Jewish people. The Hasmonaeans not only reclaimed the Temple in Jerusalem and restored Jewish worship, but they also established an independent Jewish state that lasted for over a century.

This book examines the political, religious, and social aspects of the Hasmonaeans and their legacy. It explores the rise and fall of the Hasmonaean dynasty, from the leadership of Judah Maccabee to the eventual takeover by the Romans in 63 BC. It also delves into the emergence of two important sects in Jewish history, the Pharisees and the Sadducees, and how their ideologies and practices were shaped by the Hasmonaeans.

The Maccabees: The Hasmonaeans Dynasty between Malachi and Matthew also explores the impact of the Hasmonaeans on the formation of Jewish identity, the development of Jewish law, and the emergence of key figures in the New Testament. The book also examines the political and military campaigns of the Hasmonaeans and their impact on the Jewish people and their neighboring nations.

This book is an essential resource for scholars, students, and anyone interested in understanding the complex history of ancient Judaism and its impact on the formation of religious sects and the emergence of key figures in the New Testament. The Maccabees: The Hasmonaeans Dynasty between Malachi and Matthew provides a detailed and nuanced perspective on the Hasmonaeans and their legacy, shedding light on a critical period of Jewish history that has often been overlooked in broader historical narratives.

The book draws on a wide range of primary and secondary sources, including the writings of Josephus, the Dead Sea Scrolls, and the Apocryphal books of the Maccabees. It is written in an accessible style that makes it suitable for both academic and general readers. The book is well-organized and easy to navigate, making it an ideal resource for scholars, students, and anyone interested in understanding the complex history of ancient Judaism.

In conclusion, The Maccabees: The Hasmonaeans Dynasty between Malachi and Matthew is a comprehensive, engaging, and informative study of the Hasmonaeans dynasty, which provides readers with an in-depth understanding of the political, religious and social aspects of the Hasmonaeans and their legacy. It is an essential resource for scholars, students and general readers interested in the history of ancient Judaism.

CHAPTER 1 Who Were the Maccabees?

The Maccabees were a Jewish rebel group that fought against the Seleucid Empire in the 2nd century BC. They were led by the priest Mattathias and his five sons, the most famous of whom was Judas Maccabeus. The Maccabees were able to defeat the Seleucids and establish an independent Jewish kingdom known as the Hasmonean dynasty. The Maccabean Revolt is celebrated in the Jewish holiday of Hanukkah.

The Maccabees were able to defeat the Seleucid forces in a series of battles, and in 164 BC they were able to reclaim the Temple in Jerusalem, which had been desecrated by the Seleucids. This event is celebrated in the Jewish holiday of Hanukkah.

With the Temple reclaimed and the Seleucid Empire driven out of the area, the Maccabees established an independent Jewish kingdom known as the Hasmonean dynasty. The Hasmoneans ruled for over a century, until 63 BC, when the Roman Republic conquered the area and made it a province of the Roman Empire.

Throughout their history, the Maccabees were able to maintain Jewish religious and cultural traditions, and they are remembered as great defenders of the Jewish people. The Maccabean Revolt is an important event in Jewish history and an inspiration for Jewish nationalism movements throughout history.

How did they affect Judaism before the coming of the foretold Messiah?

The Maccabees played a significant role in shaping Judaism before the coming of the foretold Messiah.

Firstly, the Maccabees were able to reclaim the Temple in Jerusalem and rededicate it to the worship of God. This event, known as the "Miracle of the Oil," is celebrated in the Jewish holiday of Hanukkah and is seen as a major victory for the Jewish people and their religious traditions.

Secondly, the Maccabees established an independent Jewish kingdom, the Hasmonean dynasty, which allowed for the preservation of Jewish religious and cultural traditions. The Hasmoneans, who were also priests, emphasized the importance of Jewish religious law and the study of the Torah, which helped to solidify the foundations of Judaism as a religion.

Thirdly, the Hasmoneans expanded the boundaries of the Jewish state and this led to the spread of Judaism and the conversion of many people to the faith.

Lastly, the Maccabees paved the way for the emergence of the Pharisees, a sect that developed around the time of the Hasmonean dynasty, which would later become one of the most influential Jewish sects before the coming of the Messiah.

Overall, the Maccabees played a vital role in preserving and strengthening Jewish religious and cultural traditions, and their legacy continues to be felt in the Jewish religion to this day.

How were the Jews in Israel affected by Hellenistic rule?

The Jews in Israel were affected by Hellenistic rule in a number of ways.

Firstly, the Seleucid Empire, which controlled Israel after the death of Alexander the Great, attempted to impose Greek culture and religion on the Jewish population. This included efforts to build Greek-style temples and to encourage the adoption of Greek customs and practices. This led to a significant amount of cultural assimilation among the Jewish population, and many Jews began to adopt Greek ways of life.

Secondly, the Seleucid Empire also attempted to suppress Jewish religious practices. This included prohibiting the practice of Jewish rituals, such as circumcision, and banning the study of Jewish religious texts. They also tried to force the Jewish population to participate in Greek religious practices and festivals.

Thirdly, the Seleucid Empire also imposed heavy taxes on the Jewish population, which caused significant economic hardship.

All these efforts led to a growing sense of resentment among the Jewish population and eventually led to the Maccabean Revolt, where the Jewish people, led by the Maccabees, rose up against Seleucid rule, and were able to reclaim the Temple in Jerusalem, establish an independent Jewish kingdom and preserve Jewish religious and cultural traditions.

Corruption of the Priests

The corruption of the priests was one of the most significant ways in which Hellenistic influence manifested among the Jews. Many priests, eager to modernize and progress with the times, saw the incorporation of Hellenistic elements into Judaism as a way to do so. One such individual was Jason, the brother of the high priest Onias III.

While Onias was away in Antioch, Jason bribed the Greek authorities in order to secure appointment as high priest, in place of Onias. The Seleucid ruler Antiochus Epiphanes, who was in need of funds for military campaigns, accepted the bribe and granted Jerusalem the status of a Greek city, or "polis". Jason then built a gymnasium in

Jerusalem, where young Jews and even priests could compete in Greek games.

However, this act of treachery led to further corruption and treachery. Three years later, Menelaus, who may not have been of the priestly line, offered an even higher bribe to Antiochus, and Jason was forced to flee. Menelaus then took large sums of money from the temple treasury to pay Antiochus, and arranged the murder of Onias III, who had spoken out against this theft.

When rumors spread that Antiochus had died, Jason returned to Jerusalem with a thousand men in an attempt to reclaim the high priesthood from Menelaus. But Antiochus was not dead, and upon hearing of Jason's actions and the growing resistance to his Hellenization policies among the Jews, he responded with a vengeance. This incident highlights how the pursuit of power and wealth can lead to the erosion of religious and cultural traditions and how the actions of individuals can have far-reaching consequences for an entire community.

Antiochus Takes Action

In his book The Maccabees, historian Moshe Pearlman suggests that Antiochus Epiphanes, the Seleucid ruler, came to the conclusion that allowing the Jews religious autonomy was a political mistake. He believed that the rebellion in Jerusalem was not solely motivated by religious factors, but also by pro-Egyptian sentiments among the Jews, which were able to flourish precisely because of the Jews' religious separatism. As a result, Antiochus decided to suppress Jewish religious practices and customs.

Israeli statesman and scholar Abba Eban describes the events that followed: Antiochus ordered the massacre of Jews, looting of the Temple, and the prohibition of Jewish religious practices. Circumcision and Sabbath observance were punishable by death. The ultimate insult came in December 167 BC, when Antiochus ordered the construction of an altar to Zeus within the Temple and the sacrifice of pigs, which are considered unclean by Jewish law. This period saw the continuation of Hellenized Jews like Menelaus in their positions, officiating at the now defiled Temple.

While many Jews accepted Hellenism, a new group called the Hasidim, or pious ones, emerged, encouraging stricter adherence to the Law of Moses. The common people, now disillusioned with the Hellenized priests, began to side more and more with the Hasidim. A period of martyrdom ensued, as Jews throughout the country were forced to either conform to pagan customs and sacrifices or face death. The apocryphal books of the Maccabees provide accounts of men, women, and children who chose death over compromise during this time. Antiochus's actions were a turning point that led to the Maccabean Revolt and the establishment of the independent Jewish kingdom. The events of this period were a stark reminder of the importance of religious freedom and the dangers of forced assimilation and cultural suppression.

The Maccabees React

The Maccabean Revolt was a significant event in Jewish history, sparked by the oppressive actions of Antiochus IV Epiphanes, the ruler of the Seleucid Empire. The Greek king sought to impose Greek culture and religion on the Jewish people, including the forced worship of Greek gods. In response, a Jewish priest named Mattathias from the town of Modi'in, located northwest of Jerusalem, took a stand against the king's representatives when they demanded that he participate in a pagan sacrifice. Enraged by the compromise of another Jew, Mattathias killed both the Greek official and the other Jew. This act of defiance inspired the residents of Modi'in and other Jews, including the Hasidim, to join Mattathias in his rebellion against Greek rule. Mattathias appointed his son Judah, also known as Judah Maccabee, as the leader of the military operations, and the family became known as the Maccabees. The Maccabees were successful in their rebellion and were able to reclaim Jerusalem and the Temple, which is celebrated in the Jewish holiday of Hanukkah.

The Temple Reclaimed

The Maccabean Revolt, led by Mattathias and his sons, including Judah Maccabee, was a significant moment in Jewish history as it marked the beginning of Jewish autonomy and religious freedom. During the early stages of the revolt, Mattathias, who was viewed as a religious authority, made the decision to allow Jews to defend themselves on the Sabbath, which gave new life to the rebellion and set a precedent in Judaism for religious leaders to adapt Jewish law to changing circumstances.

After the death of his father, Judah Maccabee became the undisputed leader of the rebellion and employed guerrilla warfare tactics to defeat the larger and better-equipped Seleucid army. He was able to capture strategic locations and gain control of Jerusalem successfully. In December 165 BC, or perhaps 164 BC, Judah and his troops captured the Temple, cleansed its utensils, and rededicated it.

The Maccabees' success in reclaiming the Temple was a significant moment in Jewish history as it allowed the Jewish people to practice their religion once again freely and restore their sense of identity and cultural heritage. The story of the Maccabees and the reclaiming of the Temple is told in the books of 1 and 2 Maccabees and is still remembered and honored. The Maccabees' achievement also shows the importance of religious leaders adapting Jewish law to changing circumstances, which is reflected in later Jewish religious texts such as the Talmud.

Politics Over Piety

The Maccabean Revolt, led by the Maccabee brothers and initially sparked by the oppressive actions of the Seleucid Empire against the Jewish people, was successful in achieving its initial goals of removing prohibitions against the practice of Judaism and restoring worship and sacrifices at the Temple. However, the goals of the rebellion shifted as the Maccabees began to focus on establishing an independent Jewish state. The religious motivations that had initially sparked the revolt were replaced by political incentives, and the struggle for autonomy continued.

Judah Maccabee, after becoming the leader of the rebellion, sought support in his fight against Seleucid domination by forming a treaty with Rome. Despite his death in battle, his brothers continued the fight and Jonathan, one of the brothers, was able to maneuver a situation in which he was appointed as high priest and ruler in Judea, though still under Seleucid sovereignty. Eventually, under the leadership of Simeon Maccabee, the last vestiges of Seleucid domination were removed and an independent Hasmonaean dynasty was established, with the Maccabees in power.

The Maccabees were able to reestablish worship at the Temple before the coming of the Messiah, but their rule as politically-minded priests rather than a king of David's line did not bring true blessings to the Jewish people. The actions of the Hellenized priests and the Hasmonaeans, the dynasty founded by the Maccabees, further shook the confidence in the priesthood and did not bring true stability to the Jewish people

The Maccabees continued to fight against the Seleucid Empire and were able to establish Jewish autonomy and religious freedom. Under the leadership of Judah Maccabee and his brothers, the Maccabees defeated the Seleucid army in several major battles and reconquered Jerusalem and the Temple. They then rededicated the Temple in 164 BC, an event that is commemorated in the Jewish holiday of Hanukkah.

After Judah's death, his brother Jonathan assumed leadership and continued to expand Jewish territory and strengthen the Jewish state. The Hasmonean dynasty, founded by the Maccabees, ruled Judea for over a century and made significant contributions to Jewish culture and religious practice. However, internal conflicts and political rivalries eventually led to the decline of the Hasmonean dynasty and the rise of Roman rule in the region.

CHAPTER 2 The Hasmonaeans and Their Legacy

During the time of Jesus, Judaism was characterized by a diversity of factions vying for influence over the population. The New Testament Gospels and the writings of the Jewish historian Josephus both attest to this fact, with groups such as the Pharisees and Sadducees being particularly prominent in this regard. However, these groups are not mentioned in the Hebrew Scriptures. Josephus first mentions the Sadducees and Pharisees in the context of the second century BC, a period marked by increased influence of Greek culture and philosophy, known as Hellenism, on Jewish society. This tension between Hellenism and Judaism reached a climax when the Seleucid rulers desecrated the temple in Jerusalem, dedicating it to the Greek god Zeus. The Hasmonaean family, led by the charismatic Judah Maccabee, successfully led a rebellion against the Seleucids, freeing the temple and restoring Jewish worship.

Following the Maccabean victory, a trend towards the formation of sects based on competing ideologies emerged, with each group vying to win over the wider Jewish community. This development raises the question of why Judaism became so divided. To understand this phenomenon, it is important to examine the history and legacy of the Hasmonaeans. The Hasmonaeans were a family of Jewish leaders who played a pivotal role in shaping the political and religious landscape of ancient Israel during the Second Temple period. Their legacy has had a profound and lasting impact on Jewish history and culture.

Increasing Independence and Disunity

After successfully restoring worship at the Temple of Jehovah, Judah Maccabee shifted his focus to politics, which led to many Jews distancing themselves from him. Nevertheless, he continued to fight against the Seleucid rulers, formed alliances with Rome, and aimed to establish an independent Jewish state. Following Judah's death in battle, his brothers Jonathan and Simon carried on the struggle. Initially, the Seleucid rulers opposed the Maccabees fiercely, but over time, they agreed to a political compromise, granting the Hasmonaean brothers a degree of autonomy.

However, many Jews felt that the position of high priest, which had never been held by a Hasmonaean, should be filled by priests of the line of Zadok, as appointed by King Solomon. Jonathan used a combination of warfare and diplomacy to persuade the Seleucids to appoint him as high priest. After Jonathan's death, his brother Simon achieved even more; in September 140 BC, a crucial decree was issued in Jerusalem, which recognized Simon as high priest and leader of the Jewish people, a position that would be passed down to his descendants. This marked a significant turning point, as historian Emil Schürer noted, the Hasmonaeans' primary concern shifted from fulfilling the Jewish Law to maintaining and expanding their political power. Simon employed the title "ethnarch," or "leader of the people," rather than "king" to avoid offending Jewish sensibilities.

However, not everyone was pleased with the Hasmonaeans' control over both religious and political matters. According to many scholars, it was during this period that the Qumran community was formed. A priest of the line of Zadok, believed to be the one referred to in Qumran writings as "the Teacher of Righteousness," left Jerusalem and led an opposition group into the Judean Desert by the Dead Sea. Many scholars believe that either Jonathan or Simon could fit the sect's description of the ruling "Wicked Priest." Simon continued military campaigns to expand the territory under his control, but his rule came to an abrupt end when his son-in-law, Ptolemy, assassinated him along with two of his sons while they were banqueting near Jericho. This attempt at gaining control failed, and John Hyrcanus, Simon's remaining son, captured his potential assassins and took over the leadership and high priesthood in place of his father.

Further Expansion and Oppression

Upon taking leadership, John Hyrcanus initially faced significant challenges from Syrian forces. However, in 129 BC, the Seleucid dynasty suffered a decisive defeat at the hands of the Parthians, resulting in the collapse of the Seleucid kingdom. This allowed Hyrcanus to fully restore Judea's political independence and to embark on a campaign of territorial expansion. Unencumbered by any Syrian threat, Hyrcanus began to invade and subjugate territories beyond Judea, forcing their inhabitants to convert to Judaism or face the destruction of their cities. One notable example of this was his campaign against the Idumaeans (Edomites), which resulted in the forced conversion of an entire race, rather than just a few individuals. Additionally, Hyrcanus conquered and razed the Samaritan temple on Mount Gerazim.

This policy of forced conversion by the Hasmonaean dynasty contradicts the principle of religious freedom, which the previous generation, led by Judah Maccabee, had fought to defend. It is a striking irony that a grandson of Mattathias, Judah Maccabee's father, would violate this principle. Historian Solomon Grayzel pointed out this irony in his writings. These actions of Hyrcanus and Hasmonaean dynasty drew criticisms from scholars and historians for the oppression of other religious groups and forced conversion.

Pharisees and Sadducees Appear

It was during the reign of John Hyrcanus that the influence of the Pharisees and the Sadducees began to increase, as noted by the Jewish historian Josephus. Although Josephus does not provide information on the origins of these groups, some scholars believe they emerged from the Hasidim, a sect of pious individuals who supported Judah Maccabee's religious goals but withdrew their support when his ambitions turned political. The name Pharisees is generally associated with the Hebrew root meaning "separate ones," although it could also be related to the word "interpreters." They were scholars from among the common people, with no special descent, who separated themselves from ritual impurities by a philosophy of special piety, applying temple laws of priestly holiness to everyday life. They developed a new method of interpreting Scriptures and a concept known as the oral law. They gained greater influence during Simon's reign, with some being appointed to the Gerousia, which later became known as the Sanhedrin.

However, Josephus reports that John Hyrcanus was initially a pupil and supporter of the Pharisees, but their relationship broke down when the Pharisees criticized him for not giving up the high priesthood.

As a result, Hyrcanus outlawed the Pharisees' religious ordinances and aligned himself with their opponents, the Sadducees. The name Sadducees is likely connected to the High Priest Zadok, whose descendants held the priestly office since the time of King Solomon. However, not all Sadducees were of this line. According to Josephus, the Sadducees were the aristocrats and wealthy individuals of the nation, and they did not have the support of the masses. Professor Schiffman notes that "most of them...were apparently priests or those who had intermarried with the high priestly families." They had long been closely connected to those in power, and the increasing role of the Pharisees in public life and the Pharisaic concept of extending priestlike sanctity to all the people was perceived as a threat that could undermine the Sadducees' natural authority. In the final years of Hyrcanus' reign, the Sadducees regained control.

In summary, the Pharisees were scholars among the common people who separated themselves from ritual impurities and applied temple laws of priestly holiness to everyday life. They gained greater influence during Simon's reign and were appointed to the Gerousia. On the other hand, the Sadducees were the aristocrats and wealthy individuals of the nation, and they did not have the support of the masses. They were closely connected to those in power and were opposed to the Pharisees' increasing influence in public life, which they perceived as a threat to their traditional authority. The Pharisees and Sadducees both emerged during the time of John Hyrcanus reign, and their rise was closely tied to the political and religious developments of the time. Hyrcanus initially supported the Pharisees, but their relationship broke down, leading him to outlaw their religious ordinances and align himself with the Sadducees. The Sadducees regained control in the final years of Hyrcanus' reign.

More Politics, Less Piety

Under the reign of Alexander Jannaeus, the Hasmonaean dynasty reached the peak of its power. He broke with previous policy and declared himself both high priest and king. This led to increased conflicts with the Pharisees and even a civil war in which 50,000 Jews died. Jannaeus quelled the rebellion by having 800 of the rebels impaled, an act that was reminiscent of pagan kings. He also ordered the slaughter of the wives and children of the impaled rebels in front of them while he feasted with his concubines. Despite his hostility towards the Pharisees, Jannaeus was a pragmatic politician and recognized their increasing popular support.

Before his death, Jannaeus instructed his wife, Salome Alexandra, to share power with the Pharisees. Salome Alexandra proved to be a capable ruler and provided the nation with one of the more peaceful periods under Hasmonaean rule. She restored the Pharisees to positions of authority and revoked the laws against their religious ordinances.

However, after Salome's death, her sons Hyrcanus II and Aristobulus II entered into a power struggle. Both lacked the political and military insight of their forefathers and neither fully understood the significance of the increasing Roman presence in the area after the collapse of the Seleucid kingdom. In 63 BC, both brothers turned to the Roman ruler Pompey for mediation in their dispute. That same year, Pompey and his troops marched into Jerusalem and took control. This marked the beginning of the end for the Hasmonaean kingdom. In 37 BC, Jerusalem was taken over by the Idumaean King Herod the Great, whom the Roman Senate had approved as "King of Judea," "ally and friend of the Roman people." The Hasmonaean kingdom was no more.

The Hasmonaean Dynasty

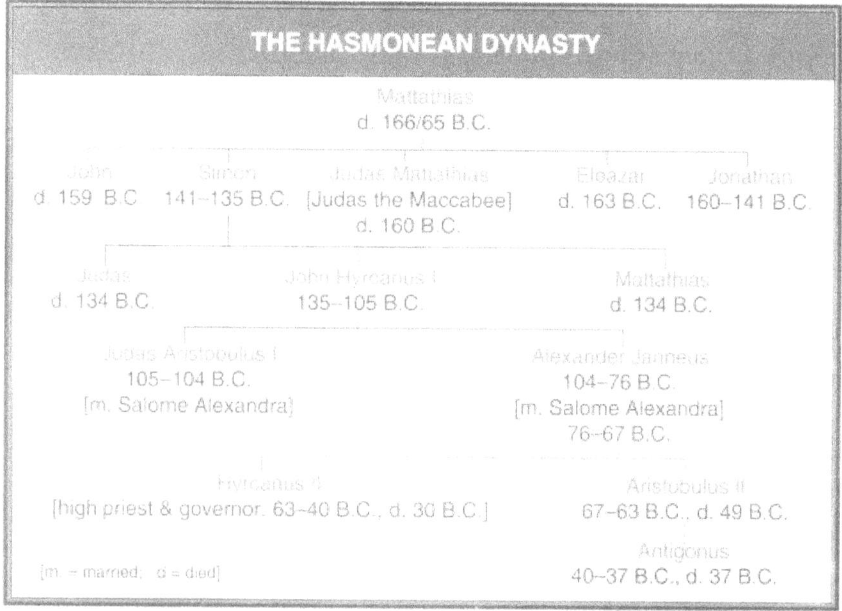

Image 1 David S. Dockery et al., Holman Bible Handbook (Nashville, TN: Holman Bible Publishers, 1992), 512.

CHAPTER 3 Mattathias ben Johanan

Image 2 Mattathias, the father of Judah Maccabee, cried out: 'Let everyone who is zealous for the Law follow me'

Mattathias ben Johanan, also known as Mattathias the Hasmonean, was a Jewish priest and leader who played a crucial role in sparking the Maccabean Revolt against the Hellenistic Seleucid Empire. He is considered a hero in Jewish history and is celebrated in the festival of Hanukkah.

Background

The Seleucid Empire, which controlled the area of Israel at the time, sought to impose Greek culture and religion on the Jewish population. This included attempts to force the Jewish people to worship Greek gods, and to adopt Greek customs and practices. Mattathias and his family were among the Jewish priests who refused to comply with these demands.

Role in the Maccabean Revolt

In 167 BC, a Seleucid official arrived in the village of Modiin, where Mattathias lived, to enforce the decrees of the Seleucid king, Antiochus IV Epiphanes. The official ordered the villagers to offer a sacrifice to the Greek gods. When a Jewish collaborator stepped forward to perform the sacrifice, Mattathias became enraged and killed both the collaborator and the Seleucid official. He then called on his fellow Jews to rise up against the Seleucid Empire and to defend their faith and traditions.

Mattathias and his five sons, including Judas Maccabeus, then led the rebellion against the Seleucids. They were initially outnumbered and outmatched, but they were able to defeat the Seleucid army in a series of guerrilla warfare. Mattathias died in 166 BC, but his sons continued to lead the rebellion. The Maccabees were finally able to reclaim the Temple in Jerusalem in 164 BC, and they rededicated it to God, an event that is celebrated in the Jewish festival of Hanukkah.

Legacy

The Maccabean Revolt, led by Mattathias and his family, was a significant moment in Jewish history. It marked the end of the Seleucid Empire's attempts to impose Greek culture and religion on the Jewish people and the beginning of a period of Jewish independence.

Mattathias is remembered as a hero who stood up for his faith and his people, and his legacy is celebrated in the annual observance of Hanukkah.

Additionally, the Hasmonean dynasty, founded by Mattathias's descendants, ruled Israel for over a century, the last dynasty of Jewish priest-kings. They expanded Jewish territory, rebuilt the Temple, and established a central government and army, which helped secure Jewish independence. This dynasty also played a significant role in shaping the development of Judaism in the Second Temple period.

In conclusion, Mattathias ben Johanan was a key figure in the Maccabean Revolt, which was a pivotal moment in Jewish history. His actions sparked a rebellion against the Seleucid Empire, which sought to impose Greek culture and religion on the Jewish population. His leadership, along with that of his sons, ultimately led to Jewish independence, the rededication of the Temple in Jerusalem and the establishment of the Hasmonean dynasty. His legacy is still celebrated today, in the festival of Hanukkah.

CHAPTER 4 Judas Maccabeus

Image 3 Judah Maccabee sought Jewish independence – The Triumph of Judas Maccabeus, Rubens

Judah Maccabee (Hebrew: יהודה המכבי) was a Jewish priest and a warrior who led the Maccabean Revolt against the Seleucid Empire in the 2nd century BC. He was the third son of Mattathias the Hasmonean, a Jewish priest from the village of Modi'in. In 167 BC, Mattathias and his sons, including Judah, rose up against the Seleucid ruler Antiochus IV Epiphanes, who had issued decrees that forbade Jewish religious practices. Upon Mattathias' death in 166 BC, Judah assumed leadership of the rebellion and quickly proved himself a skilled and brave commander. He and his brothers were able to defeat the Seleucid army and reclaim Jerusalem, ultimately leading to the establishment of an independent Jewish state. The story of Judah Maccabee and the Maccabean Revolt is commemorated in the Jewish holiday of Hanukkah.

Origin of the name "The Hammer"

The origin of the name "The Hammer" for Judah Maccabee is uncertain, but it is believed to be derived from the Aramaic word "maqqaba," meaning "hammer" or "sledgehammer." This name may have been given to him in recognition of his ferocity in battle, or it could be in reference to his weapon of choice. Another theory is that the name "Maccabee" is an acronym of the verse "Mi kamokha ba'elim Adonai," meaning "Who among the gods is like you, O Lord?" which was used as a battle cry to motivate troops. Some scholars also suggest that the name is a shortened form of the Hebrew "maqqab-Yahu" meaning "the one designated by Yahweh." The name "Maccabee" was originally exclusive to Judah, but later came to signify all the Hasmoneans who fought during the Maccabean Revolt.

Early Victories

During the early stages of the Jewish revolt against the Seleucid Empire, the leader of the rebellion, Judah, employed a strategy of guerrilla warfare in order to avoid direct engagements with the superior Seleucid army. This tactic allowed Judah to score a series of victories against Seleucid forces. One notable battle was the battle of Nahal el-Haramiah, where Judah defeated a smaller Seleucid force under the command of Apollonius, the governor of Samaria, and took possession of Apollonius's sword as a symbol of vengeance. Following this victory, more individuals joined the Jewish cause. Additionally, Judah won a larger battle against the Seleucid army led by Seron near Beth-Horon, and another against the Seleucid forces led by generals Nicanor and Gorgias in the Battle of Emmaus. These victories led the Seleucid viceroy, Lysias, to assemble a new and larger army to march on Judea. After several years of conflict, Judah was able to drive out the Seleucid forces from Jerusalem, with the exception of a garrison in the citadel of Acra. He also purified the defiled Temple of Jerusalem and restored religious services on the 25th of Kislev, which became a permanent Jewish holiday known as Hanukkah, which is still celebrated to this day. The liberation of Jerusalem was a significant step towards Jewish independence.

Image 4 Judah from Die Bibel in Bildern

After Jerusalem

After the liberation of Jerusalem, Judah Maccabee and his followers faced new challenges as neighboring Greek cities attacked Jewish communities in Gilead, Transjordan, and Galilee. In response, Judah sent his brother Simeon to lead an army of 3,000 to defend the Jewish settlements in Galilee and was successful in achieving multiple victories. He also personally led a campaign in Transjordan, along with his brother Jonathan, and was able to defeat the Transjordanian tribes and save Jewish communities in fortified towns in Gilead. The Jewish population of these areas was evacuated to Judea. Following this, Judah turned his attention to the Edomites in the south, capturing and destroying the cities of Hebron and Maresha. He then marched on the coast of the Mediterranean, destroying the altars and statues of pagan gods in Ashdod, before returning to Judea with much spoils.

Image 5 Maccabean Revolt - Judea under Judah Maccabee

Judah then laid siege to the Seleucid garrison at the Acra, the Seleucid citadel in Jerusalem. The Seleucid viceroy, Lysias, responded by leading a new campaign to Judea with the young king Antiochus V Eupator. In the Battle of Beth-zechariah, south of Bethlehem, the Seleucids achieved their first major victory over the Maccabees and Judah was forced to withdraw to Jerusalem. Lysias laid siege to the city, but the defenders were able to hold out due to the outbreak of a rebellion led by Philip, the commander-in-chief appointed by the late king Antiochus Epiphanes, which forced Lysias and Eupator to withdraw. In the end, a peaceful settlement was reached, granting the Jews religious freedom, the ability to live according to their own laws, and the official return of the Temple to Jewish control. The new Seleucid ruler Demetrius appointed Alcimus, a Hellenistic Jew, as high priest, which was a controversial move among traditional Jewish factions.

Image 6 Judas Maccabeus before the army of Nicanor, by Gustave Doré

THE MACCABEES

As the war against the Seleucid Empire came to an end, an internal conflict emerged within the Jewish community between the traditionalist party led by Judah Maccabee and the Hellenizer party, which had sought to adopt Greek culture and customs. The Hellenizers had held significant influence during Seleucid rule, but their power collapsed with the defeat of the Seleucids. The Hellenizing High Priest Menelaus was removed from office and executed, and his successor, Alcimus, was also a Hellenizer. Alcimus's execution of sixty priests who opposed him led to open conflict with the Maccabees. Alcimus fled to the Seleucid king for help.

At this time, Demetrius I Soter, the son of Seleucus IV Philopator and nephew of the late Antiochus IV Epiphanes, arrived in Syria and declared himself the rightful king. He captured and killed Lysias and Antiochus Eupator and took the throne. Alcimus and his supporters then approached Demetrius with complaints of persecution by the traditionalist party in Judea. Demetrius appointed Alcimus as High Priest and sent an army led by Bacchides to support him. However, the Jewish army was unable to resist and withdrew from Jerusalem, and Judah returned to a strategy of guerrilla warfare. The Seleucid army was forced to return to Antioch due to political turmoil, and Judah's forces retook Jerusalem. The Seleucids then sent another army, led by Nicanor, which was defeated in a battle near Adasa, and Nicanor was killed. This victory was commemorated annually as the "Day of Nicanor."

In Summary: After the liberation of Jerusalem, Judah Maccabee and his followers faced new issues such as the attacks on Jewish communities in Gilead, Transjordan, and Galilee by neighboring Greek cities. This prompted Judah to send his brother Simeon to lead an army in defense of these settlements and also led him to personally lead a campaign in Transjordan to protect Jewish communities there. Additionally, an internal conflict emerged within the Jewish community between the traditionalist party led by Judah Maccabee and the Hellenizer party, which had sought to adopt Greek culture and customs. This led to open conflict, with the Hellenizer party seeking help from the Seleucid king and ultimately resulted in the Seleucid king

Demetrius I Soter sending an army to Jerusalem to support the Hellenizer party.

Agreement with Rome and Death

Image 7 Death of Judas Maccabeus by José Teófilo de Jesus

The Roman-Jewish Treaty was a historical agreement made between Judah Maccabee and the Roman Republic in 161 BC. It was the first recorded contract between the Jewish people and the Romans. However, despite this agreement, Demetrius I Soter, the Seleucid king, continued his efforts to defeat the Jewish rebellion. After receiving news of the defeat of Nicanor, Demetrius sent another army led by Bacchides, which was numerically superior to the Jewish forces. Many of Judah's men left the battlefield, and some advised him to do the same and wait for a more favorable opportunity. However, Judah decided to remain and fight. In the Battle of Elasa, Judah and his remaining followers were killed. His brothers retrieved his body and buried him in the family sepulchre at Modiin. The death of Judah Maccabee sparked renewed resistance, and after several more years of war under the leadership of two of Mattathias' other sons, Jonathan and Simon, the Jews were able to achieve independence and the freedom to worship as they chose.

CHAPTER 5 The Maccabean Revolt

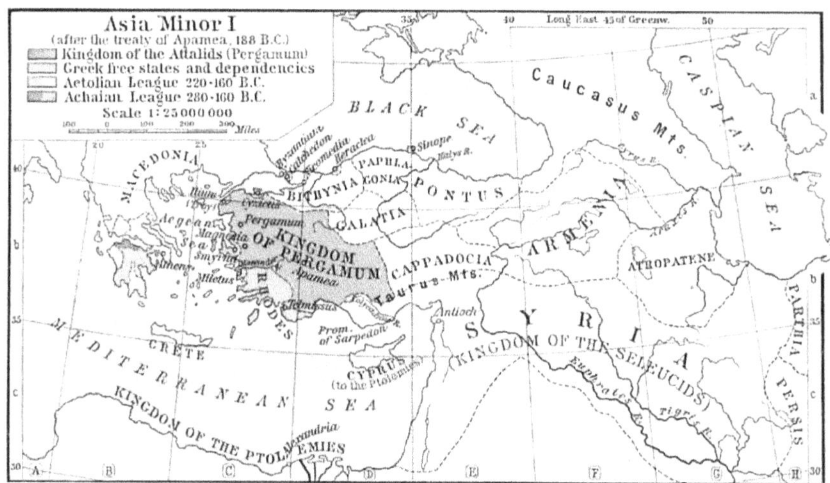

Image 8 Maccabean Revolt. (2023, January 4). In Wikipedia.
https://en.wikipedia.org/wiki/Maccabean_Revolt

The Maccabean Revolt, also known as the Hasmonean Revolt, was a Jewish rebellion led by the Maccabees against the Seleucid Empire during the 2nd century BC. The revolt began in 167 BC, sparked by the Seleucid King Antiochus IV Epiphanes' campaign of repression against the Jewish religion and culture, which included the banning of Jewish practices, the imposition of a syncretic pagan-Jewish cult in the Second Temple in Jerusalem, and the placing of the city under direct Seleucid control.

The Maccabees, led by Judas Maccabeus and his family, began a guerrilla movement in the Judean countryside, raiding towns and targeting Greek officials far from direct Seleucid control. The rebellion gradually developed into a proper army, and in 164 BC, the Maccabees captured Jerusalem, a significant early victory. The cleansing of the temple and rededication of the altar, which occurred on the 25th of Kislev, is the source of the festival of Hanukkah.

Despite the Seleucids' eventual concession of unbanned Judaism, the Maccabees, motivated by the desire for a more direct break with Seleucid rule, continued to fight for independence. Judas Maccabeus died in 160 BC in the Battle of Elasa against the Greek general Bacchides, but remnants of the Maccabees under the leadership of Judas' brother, Jonathan Apphus, continued to resist from the countryside.

It wasn't until 141 BC that Simon Thassi, the last of the Maccabean brothers, succeeded in expelling the Greeks from their citadel in Jerusalem and establishing an independent Hasmonean kingdom. The Maccabean Revolt had a significant impact on Jewish nationalism, serving as an example of a successful campaign to establish political independence and resist governmental suppression of Jewish culture and religion. The alliance with the Roman Republic helped to guarantee their independence.

Background

In 338 BC, Alexander the Great began his invasion of the Persian Empire, and by 333-332 BC, he had conquered the Levant and Palestine, which at the time was home to many Jewish exiles who had returned from Babylon due to the Persians. After Alexander's death in 323 BC, the territory was given to the Ptolemaic Egypt. The Seleucid Empire, another Greek successor state, would later conquer Judea from Egypt during a series of campaigns from 235-198 BC.

During Ptolemaic and Seleucid rule, many Jews learned Koine Greek, particularly upper-class Jews seeking favor with the government and Jewish minorities in towns that were further afield from Jerusalem and more attached to Greek trading networks. Greek philosophical ideas also spread throughout Palestine. A Greek translation of the scriptures, the Septuagint, was created during the third century BC. Many Jews also adopted dual names with both a Greek name and a Hebrew name, such as Jason and Joshua. Despite this, many Jews continued to speak the Aramaic language, which was spoken during the Babylonian exile. In general, Greek policy during this time period was to allow Jews to manage their own affairs and not to interfere with religious matters. Greek authors in the third century BC who wrote about Judaism did so mostly positively, and cultural change was largely driven by Jews themselves who were inspired by ideas from abroad; Greek rulers did not undertake explicit programs of forced Hellenization.

Image 9 A 14th century Christian work depicting Antiochus IV praying to a horned idol at the Temple. The Book of Daniel describes an "abomination of desolation" being given authority over the Temple, as well as the daily offering and sacrifice ceasing.

This policy continued under Antiochus IV Epiphanes, who came to the throne of the Seleucids in 175 BC. However, Antiochus IV replaced the high priest Onias III with his brother Jason after Jason offered a large sum of money to Antiochus. Jason also sought and received permission to make Jerusalem a self-governing polis, but with Jason able to control the citizenship lists of who would be able to vote and hold political office. These changes did not immediately cause any particular complaint from the majority of the citizenry in Jerusalem, and presumably he still kept the basic Jewish laws and tenets.

However, tensions began to rise when a newcomer named Menelaus offered an even larger bribe to Antiochus IV for the position of high priest. Jason, resentful, turned against Antiochus IV; additionally, a rumor spread that Menelaus had sold golden temple artifacts to help pay for the bribe, leading to unhappiness, especially among the city council Jason had established. This conflict was largely political rather than cultural. In 170-168 BC, the Sixth Syrian War between the Seleucids and the Ptolemaic Egyptians arose, for unclear reasons. Antiochus IV led an army to attack Egypt. On his way back through Jerusalem after the successful campaign, High Priest Menelaus allegedly invited Antiochus inside the Second Temple (in violation of Jewish law), and he raided the temple treasury for 1800 talents. This ultimately led to a Jewish rebellion known as the Maccabean Revolt, which was a significant event in Jewish history, and had a great impact on Jewish nationalism as an example of a successful campaign to establish political independence and resist governmental anti-Jewish suppression.

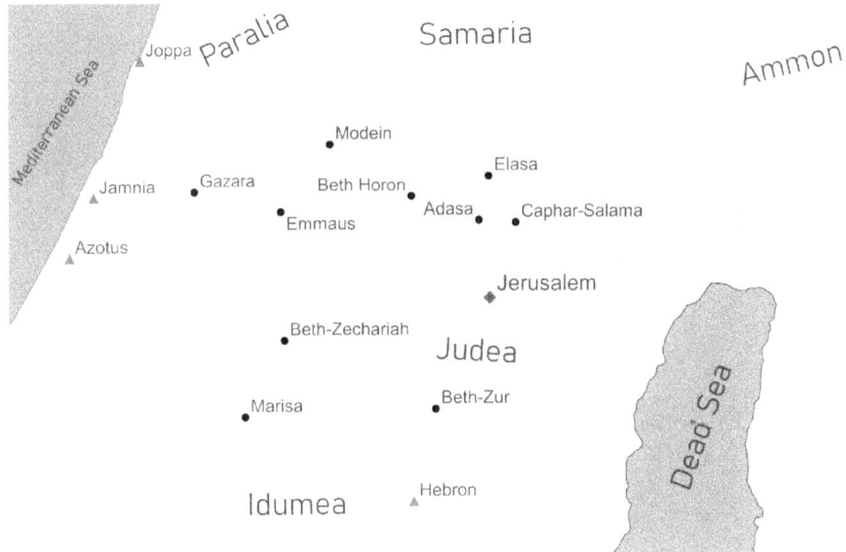

Image 10 Battles during the Maccabean Revolt. Circles mark battles against Seleucids in Judea, triangles outlying cities attacked by the Maccabees.

The Rebellion

Mattathias sparks the uprising (167 BC)

For Antiochus the unexpected conquest of the city (Jerusalem), the looting, and the wholesale slaughter were not enough. His psychopathic tendency was exacerbated by resentment at what the siege had cost him, and he tried to force the Jews to violate their traditional codes of practice by leaving their infant sons uncircumcised and sacrificing pigs on the altar. These orders were universally ignored, and Antiochus had the most prominent recusants butchered.

— *Flavius Josephus, The Jewish War, Book 1.34–35*

Image 11 Mattathias slaying the Jewish apostate, painting by Philippe De Loutherbourg

In the aftermath of Antiochus IV's decrees forbidding Jewish religious practice, a campaign of land confiscations and the construction of shrines and altars took place in the Judean countryside. A rural Jewish priest from the town of Modein, Mattathias of the Hasmonean family, sparked the revolt against the Seleucid Empire by refusing to worship the Greek gods at a newly built altar in Modein. He killed a Jew who had stepped forward to take his place in sacrificing to an idol, as well as the Greek officer who was sent to enforce the sacrifice. He then destroyed the altar. Afterward, Mattathias and his five sons fled to the nearby mountains, which sat directly next to Modein. The rebellion, led by Mattathias and his sons, was in response to the Seleucid Empire's attempts to impose their culture and religion on the Jewish population and aimed to preserve traditional Jewish culture and religion. The Maccabean Revolt ultimately resulted in the establishment of an independent Hasmonean kingdom and had a significant impact on Jewish nationalism.

Guerrilla Campaign (167–164 BC)

After the death of Mattathias in 166 BC, his son Judas Maccabeus led a band of Jewish dissidents that eventually grew into an army. They were unable to directly challenge Seleucid power, but were able to raid the countryside and attack Hellenized Jews, who were seen as collaborators. The Maccabees destroyed Greek altars in the villages, forcibly circumcised boys, burnt villages and drove Hellenized Jews off their land. They employed guerrilla tactics, using speed and mobility to their advantage. They were less trained and under-equipped for pitched battles but could control which battles they took and retreat into the wilderness when threatened. They defeated two minor Seleucid forces at the Battle of the Ascent of Lebonah in 167 BC and the Battle of Beth Horon in 166 BC. Eventually, they captured Jerusalem in 164 BC, ritually cleansed the Second Temple, reestablishing traditional Jewish worship there. The date of the cleansing in the Hebrew calendar, 25 Kislev, would later become the date when the festival of Hanukkah begins. The Seleucid Empire agreed to a political compromise that revoked Antiochus IV's ban on Jewish practices, but the Maccabees continued their campaign for a starker break from Greek influence and full political independence, which led to a loss of support from moderate Jews.

Battle of Elasa (160 BC)

In 160 BC, Seleucid King Demetrius I left his general Bacchides to govern the western part of the empire while he went on campaign in the east. Bacchides led an army of 20,000 infantry and 2,000 cavalry into Judea on a second expedition to reconquer the restive province. The size of the rebel army facing them is disputed, with some historians suspecting that the number was larger than what is stated in 1 Maccabees. The Seleucid army marched through Judea after carrying out a massacre in the Galilee. The Maccabees, led by Judas Maccabeus, encamped on the rough terrain at Elasa to intercept the Seleucid army. Judas was ultimately killed in battle, and the remaining Judeans fled. The Seleucids reasserted their authority in Jerusalem, fortifying cities across the land, putting Greek-friendly Jews in command, and ensuring that children of leading families were held as hostages. Judas's brother, Jonathan Apphus, became the new leader of the Maccabees. He continued to fight Bacchides and his troops for a time, but the two eventually made a pact for a ceasefire, and Bacchides returned to Syria in 160 BC.

Autonomy (160–138 BC)

After the defeat of Judas Maccabeus and the Seleucid's reassertion of control over Jerusalem in 160 BC, the Maccabees were able to establish a rival government in the countryside. They avoided direct conflict with the Seleucids, but continued to engage in internal Jewish civil struggles. During this time, the Seleucids were embroiled in their own civil wars, which gave the Maccabees leverage in negotiations. In 153-152 BC, a deal was struck between Jonathan Maccabee and King Demetrius I, which resulted in the withdrawal of Seleucid forces from fortified towns and garrisons in Judea, except for Beth-Zur and Jerusalem, and the release of hostages. However, Jonathan soon betrayed Demetrius I after receiving a better offer from Alexander Balas. This led to a state of informal autonomy for the Maccabees, where they were able to maintain their own army and continue to fight in the Seleucid civil wars in order to maintain the favor of Seleucid leaders. In 143 BC, Jonathan was captured and executed by a Seleucid general, but his brother Simon was able to negotiate a deal with Demetrius II Nicator, which resulted in the exemption of Judea from taxes and Simon being appointed High Priest. The Hasmoneans also established a diplomatic relationship with the Roman Republic, who officially recognized their independence in 139 BC. Simon did not immediately establish a monarchy and instead referred to himself as "nasi" or leader. The Seleucids continued to make demands for tribute and control of border towns, but the Hasmoneans were able to repulse their attempts to regain control.

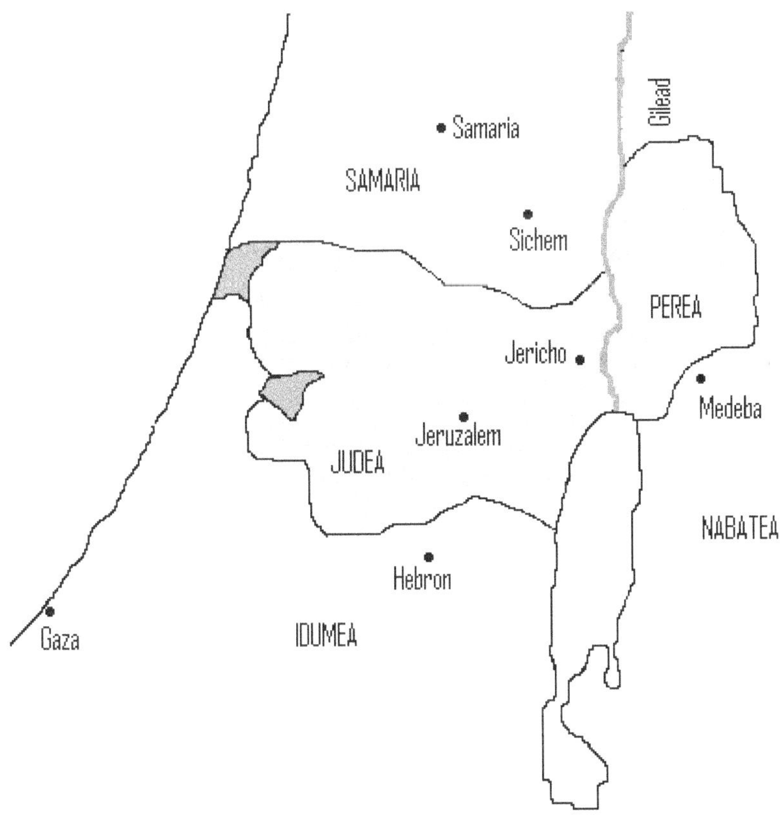

Image 12 Territory under Simon's control

In 135 BC, Simon, the leader of the Maccabees, and two of his sons were killed by his son-in-law, Ptolemy, at a feast in Jericho. This left leadership to the next generation, with Simon's third son, John Hyrcanus, becoming the new High Priest of Israel. King Antiochus VII of the Seleucid Empire would later invade and besiege Jerusalem in 134 BC, but after Hyrcanus paid a ransom and ceded control of the cities of Joppa and Gazara, the Seleucids left peacefully. This resulted in an alliance between Hyrcanus and Antiochus VII, with Antiochus making a donation of a sacrifice at the Temple. With the suzerainty briefly re-established, Judea sent troops to aid Antiochus VII in his campaigns in Persia. However, after Antiochus VII's death in 129 BC, the Hasmoneans ceased offering aid or tribute to the Seleucid Empire.

John Hyrcanus and his children centralised power more than Simon had done. Hyrcanus's son, Aristobulus I, called himself "basileus" (king) and abandoned the pretensions that the High Priest managing political matters was a temporary arrangement. The Hasmoneans exiled leaders on the council or gerusia that they felt might threaten their power. The council of elders, who would later evolve into the Sanhedrin, ceased to be an independent check on the monarchy.

The Hasmonean dynasty continued to conquer surrounding areas of Judea, especially under Alexander Jannaeus. The Seleucid Empire was too riven with internal unrest to stop this and Ptolemaic Egypt maintained friendly relations. The Hasmonean court at Jerusalem did not make a sharp break from Hellenic culture and language, and continued with a blend of Jewish traditions and Greek ones. They continued to be known by Greek names, used both Hebrew and Greek on their coinage and hired Greek mercenaries, but also restored Judaism to a place of primacy in Judea and fostered a new sense of Jewish nationalism that had sprouted during the Maccabean Revolt. The dynasty would last until 37 BC, when Herod the Great, making use of heavy Roman support, defeated the last Hasmonean ruler to become a Roman client king.

Image 13 Topographic map of Palestine at the start of the Hasmonean dynasty

Image 14 Eleazar Avaran trampled by a war elephant (illustration by Gustave Doré in 1866)

Tactics and Technology

During the Maccabean Revolt, both the Seleucid Empire and the Maccabees were influenced by Hellenistic army composition and tactics. The basic Hellenistic battle deployment consisted of heavy infantry in the center, mounted cavalry on the flanks, and mobile skirmishers in the vanguard. The most common infantry weapon used was the sarissa, a Macedonian pike that was held in two hands and had a great reach of approximately 6.3 meters, making it difficult for opponents to approach a phalanx of sarissa-wielding infantry safely. The Seleucids also had access to trained war elephants imported from India and occasionally made use of scythed chariots.

In terms of army size, historian Polybius reports that in 165 BC, a military parade near the Seleucid capital Antioch held by Antiochus IV consisted of 41,000-foot soldiers and 4,500 cavalrymen. These soldiers were preparing to fight in an expedition to the east, not in Judea, but give a rough estimate to the total size of the Seleucid forces in the Western part of their empire. The Maccabees started as a guerrilla force that likely used traditional weapons effective in small unit combat in mountainous terrains, such as archers, slingers, and light infantry peltasts armed with swords and shields. Later on, the Maccabees trained a standing army similar to the Seleucids, complete with Hellenic-style heavy infantry phalanxes, horse-mounted cavalry, and siege weaponry. In the following chapters, we will revisit these battles in greater detail.

CHAPTER 6 Battle of the Ascent of Lebonah

Image 15 Presumed location of the battle, 1912

The Battle of the Ascent of Lebonah (Hebrew: קרב מעלה לבונה), also known as the Battle with Apollonius (Hebrew: קרב אפולוניוס), was a significant military engagement that occurred in 167 or 166 BC between the Maccabees and the Seleucid Empire. The Maccabees, a Jewish rebellion group, were led by Judas Maccabeus (commonly referred to as Judah Maccabee) in this battle. On the other side, the Seleucid Empire, a Hellenistic state that controlled much of the Middle East, had Apollonius as the commanding general of their army.

This battle marked the first military encounter between the Maccabees and the Seleucid Empire, which would later be known as the Maccabean Revolt. The Maccabees, under the leadership of Judas Maccabeus, were able to defeat the Seleucid Empire in this battle, a significant achievement in their rebellion against the Greek-influenced Seleucids. According to the historian Josephus, Apollonius was described as the "strategos (general) of the Samaritan forces," indicating that the Seleucid army also had the support of the neighboring Samaritan people. The Battle of the Ascent of Lebonah was a crucial moment in Jewish history and set the stage for the Maccabean Revolt which ultimately led to the re-establishment of Jewish independence.

The Maccabean Revolt was a rebellion of the Jewish people against the Seleucid Empire, which controlled much of the Middle East at the time. At the onset of the revolt, Judas Maccabeus (also known as Judah Maccabee) led a small group of guerrilla fighters in the mountainous regions of northern Judea and southern Samaria. In response, the Seleucid Empire sent Apollonius, along with local Samaritan armies, to connect with Seleucid forces from Jerusalem.

Although the exact location of the battle is not known, it is believed to have occurred along a road between Samaria and Jerusalem. The exact date of the battle is also uncertain, but it is believed to have taken place early in the revolt. The Battle of the Ascent of Lebonah, as it is known, is the first battle discussed in the book of 1 Maccabees and is generally dated to 167-166 BC. It marks the first military engagement between the Maccabees and the Seleucid Empire, and the Maccabees were able to defeat the Seleucid forces in this battle. This was a significant achievement for the Maccabees and set the stage for further resistance and ultimately the re-establishment of Jewish independence.

While the specific details of the battle are not well-known, it is believed that the Maccabees employed guerrilla warfare tactics, such as surprise attacks and nighttime assaults. This is supported by the account of 2 Maccabees, which describes the rebels as "coming unexpectedly" on their enemies.

It is possible that the Battle of the Ascent of Lebonah was similar, with the Maccabees launching a surprise attack while the enemy was unprepared. The larger Syrian Greek army was defeated, and Judas Maccabeus, the leader of the Maccabees, defeated Apollonius in personal combat. This victory was a significant achievement for the Maccabees, which encouraged them to continue their resistance against the Seleucid Empire. The Seleucids soon sent another force against the Maccabees, which led to the Battle of Beth Horon. This battle was a continuation of the rebellion, but the Maccabees were able to defeat the Seleucid army and establish Jewish independence.

Primary Source

The battle's only contemporaneous record is in the First Book of Maccabees. According to it:

1 Maccabees 3:10-12 New Revised Standard Version, Anglicised Catholic Edition

[10] Apollonius now gathered together Gentiles and a large force from Samaria to fight against Israel. [11] When Judas learned of it, he went out to meet him, and he defeated and killed him. Many were wounded and fell, and the rest fled. [12] Then they seized their spoils; and Judas took the sword of Apollonius, and used it in battle for the rest of his life.

The Battle with Apollonius is recorded in the First Book of Maccabees, which is the only contemporaneous account of the battle. However, 2 Maccabees provides a general description of the early phase of the Maccabean Revolt, including the tactics employed by Judas Maccabeus, the leader of the Maccabees, such as surprise attacks, setting towns and villages on fire, capturing strategic positions, and fighting at night.

It is possible that the original five-volume work written by Jason of Cyrene covered the battle in more detail, but this information was condensed into a single sentence in the abridged version of 2 Maccabees. The historian Josephus also mentions the battle briefly in his book Antiquities of the Jews Book 12, Chapter 7, but appears to largely paraphrase the account provided in 1 Maccabees. Despite the limited historical records, the Battle of the Ascent of Lebonah is considered a significant event in Jewish history as it marks the first military engagement between the Maccabees and the Seleucid Empire, and the Maccabees' victory in this battle set the stage for the continuation of their rebellion and ultimately the re-establishment of Jewish independence.

Analysis

The book of 1 Maccabees provides a relatively vague account of the Battle of the Ascent of Lebonah, also known as the Battle with Apollonius, compared to the other battles in the Maccabean Revolt. The duel described in the account may be more of a scriptural reference than a historical one, as the author uses phrases and language that closely resemble those found in the story of David and Goliath in the Hebrew Bible. This literary device aligns with the author's agenda to present the Hasmoneans, the dynasty of Jewish priests and rulers who emerged after the Maccabean Revolt, as heirs to the legacy of heroes of the Hebrew Bible and to counter the claims of those in the early Hasmonean kingdom who saw the Hasmoneans as usurpers, such as the Essenes.

Historian Bezalel Bar-Kochva argues that it is unlikely that the author of the book was an eyewitness or was able to interview someone who was, unlike the later battles which are described in greater detail. He also cautions that the claims of the Seleucid force being a "large army" should be viewed with skepticism, as soldiers often overestimate the size of opposing armies, and claiming to have defeated more enemies would naturally make for a more impressive and inspiring story to rally the cause. The precise date and location of the battle are not known, but it is believed to have occurred early in the revolt, possibly between Spring 166 BC to Spring 165 BC of the Gregorian calendar, and presumably on the road between Samaria and Jerusalem. Michael Avi-Yonah proposed that an ascent near Lebonah (modern Al-Lubban ash-Sharqiya and Ma'ale Levona) was the most likely spot, halfway between Shechem (modern Nablus) and Jerusalem. The ascent there is steep and winding, with multiple places difficult to scout and thus useful for a raiding force to hide and prepare for an ambush from. Another proposal is somewhat further south at Wadi Haramiya, just north of Silwad; the road there is overlooked by ridges on both sides. The historian Josephus mentions the battle briefly and describes Apollonius as "the strategos (general) of the Samaritan forces," indicating that the Seleucid army also had the support of the neighboring Samaritan people.

Fictional Story of the Battle of the Ascent of Lebonah

Once upon a time, in the land of Judea, a group of Jewish rebels known as the Maccabees were fighting for their freedom against the powerful Seleucid Empire. The leader of the Maccabees was a brave and cunning warrior named Judas Maccabeus, who was determined to defeat the Seleucids and secure the freedom of his people.

One day, the Seleucids sent a large army led by a powerful commander named Apollonius to crush the rebellion. The Maccabees knew that they had to act quickly if they wanted to defeat the Seleucids, so Judas devised a plan to ambush the enemy at a strategic mountain pass known as the Ascent of Lebonah.

The Maccabees set up their camp at the base of the mountain and waited for the Seleucids to arrive. As the enemy approached, Judas gave a rousing speech to his troops, urging them to fight with all their might for the freedom of their people.

The Seleucids were caught off guard as the Maccabees launched a surprise attack from the mountain pass. The Maccabees were outnumbered, but they were determined and skilled fighters. They used guerrilla warfare tactics to ambush the Seleucids, catching them off guard and forcing them to retreat in confusion.

The Seleucids fought hard, but the Maccabees were able to hold their ground and push them back. Eventually, the Seleucids were defeated and forced to retreat. The Maccabees had won a decisive victory and secured the mountain pass, allowing them to continue their fight for freedom.

Judas and his Maccabees were hailed as heroes by the Jewish people, and their victory at the Ascent of Lebonah served as a powerful symbol of hope and resistance against the Seleucid Empire. The Maccabees continued to fight for their freedom and eventually established the Hasmonean kingdom.

The Battle of the Ascent of Lebonah will always be remembered as a pivotal moment in Jewish history, where a small group of rebels were able to defeat a powerful empire and pave the way for freedom and independence.

CHAPTER 7 Battle of Beth Horon (166 BC)

Image 16 Mina of Antiochus IV

The Battle of Beth Horon, also known as the Battle with Seron, took place between Spring 166 BC and Spring 165 BC during the Maccabean Revolt. The Maccabean Revolt was a rebellion against the Seleucid Empire, led by the Jewish leader Judas Maccabeus, also known as Judah Maccabee. The battle occurred at the strategic mountain pass of Beth-Horon, which connects the coastal plain to the Judean hill country.

The Maccabee rebels, using guerrilla warfare tactics, ambushed the Seleucid army led by Seron, a commander of the Syrian army, as they passed through the mountain pass. The surprise attack caught the Seleucid force off guard, causing them to flee in confusion. The Maccabee rebels then pursued the fleeing Seleucid soldiers into the plain.

Prior to the Battle of Beth Horon, the Jewish army led by Maccabeus had already won a battle at the ascent of Lebonah against the Seleucid General Apollonius. The Seleucid Empire then sent another force to combat the Maccabees, which led to the Battle of Emmaus.

The battle's only contemporaneous record is in the First Book of Maccabees. According to it:

1 Maccabees 3:13-26 New Revised Standard Version, Anglicised Catholic Edition

[13] When Seron, the commander of the Syrian army, heard that Judas had gathered a large company, including a body of faithful soldiers who stayed with him and went out to battle, [14] he said, 'I will make a name for myself and win honour in the kingdom. I will make war on Judas and his companions, who scorn the king's command.' [15] Once again a strong army of godless men went up with him to help him, to take vengeance on the Israelites.

[16] When he approached the ascent of Beth-horon, Judas went out to meet him with a small company. [17] But when they saw the army coming to meet them, they said to Judas, 'How can we, few as we are, fight against so great and so strong a multitude? And we are faint, for we have eaten nothing today.' [18] Judas replied, 'It is easy for many to be hemmed in by few, for in the sight of Heaven there is no difference between saving by many or by few. [19] It is not on the size of the army that victory in battle depends, but strength comes from Heaven. [20] They come against us in great insolence and lawlessness to destroy us and our wives and our children, and to despoil us; [21] but we fight for our lives and our laws. [22] He himself will crush them before us; as for you, do not be afraid of them.'

[23] When he finished speaking, he rushed suddenly against Seron and his army, and they were crushed before him. [24] They pursued

them down the descent of Beth-horon to the plain; eight hundred of them fell, and the rest fled into the land of the Philistines. [25] Then Judas and his brothers began to be feared, and terror fell on the Gentiles all around them. [26] His fame reached the king, and the Gentiles talked of the battles of Judas.

The historian Josephus, in his work "Antiquities of the Jews," mentions the Battle of Beth Horon, but his account appears to be largely based on a paraphrase of the version found in the book of 1 Maccabees. However, there are some notable differences in Josephus's account. For example, Josephus claims that Seron, the commander of the Seleucid army, was killed outright during the battle, whereas 1 Maccabees only states that his army was defeated. Josephus also refers to Seron as a general (strategos) rather than a commander.

Historian Bezalel Bar-Kochva suggests that Josephus may have misread 1 Maccabees when it comes to the matter of Seron's fate. While 1 Maccabees states that Seron was "defeated," Bar-Kochva believes that Josephus may have read this more literally as Seron being killed in battle. This illustrates the importance of considering the different historical sources and interpreting them critically, as different authors may have different perspectives and biases.

Analysis

The Battle of Beth Horon, as described in the historical account of the 1 Maccabees and the historian Josephus, took place in a strategically important location - the narrow pass of Beth Horon. Despite its narrowness, it was still a main road from Jerusalem to the west during that era, making it a plausible spot for a small force to inflict major damage on a larger, less coordinated enemy. The book of 1 Maccabees, in which the account of this battle is recorded, is known for its literary style, as the speeches and prayers attributed to Judas Maccabeus, the leader of the Jewish rebels, are likely free compositions of the historian rather than actual transcriptions.

The book of 1 Maccabees also makes use of archaic phrasings to present the deeds of the Hasmoneans, the family of Judas Maccabeus, as similar or equivalent to those of earlier heroes of Jewish Scripture.

The defeated Seleucid force is said to have retreated to the "land of the Philistines", which is likely a poetic reference to the eparchy of Paralia on Judea's coastal plain, which was friendly to the Greeks. The exact date of the battle is not known, but it is likely to have occurred between 166–165 BC.

Bar-Kochva, a historian, has suggested that the author of 1 Maccabees was not an eyewitness to the battle, but was able to interview someone who was. He also posits that the author may have inflated the number of enemy soldiers and Seron's rank to make the victory seem more impressive. The claim that "terror" befell the non-Jewish population in the vicinity of the battle as a result of the Maccabees' victory seems overstated, as later events in the text show that they were not so afraid as to avoid further conflicts with the Maccabees.

The identity of Seron and his "godless" allies is not entirely clear. The name "Seron" may be of Thracian origin, and his allies may have included outlying Samaritans or Ammonites, Thracian mercenaries, or even Hellenized Jews who had been recruited as soldiers by the Seleucid government.

Fictional Story of the Battle of Beth Horon

Once upon a time, in the land of Judea, a group of Jewish rebels known as the Maccabees were fighting for their freedom against the powerful Seleucid Empire. The leader of the Maccabees was a brave and cunning warrior named Judas Maccabeus, who was determined to defeat the Seleucids and secure the freedom of his people.

One day, the Seleucids sent a large army led by a powerful commander named Seron to crush the rebellion. The Maccabees knew that they had to act quickly if they wanted to defeat the Seleucids, so Judas devised a plan to ambush the enemy at a strategic mountain pass known as the Beth Horon.

The Maccabees set up their camp at the base of the mountain and waited for the Seleucids to arrive. As the enemy approached, Judas gave a rousing speech to his troops, urging them to fight with all their might for the freedom of their people.

The Seleucids were caught off guard as the Maccabees launched a surprise attack from the mountain pass. The Maccabees were outnumbered, but they were determined and skilled fighters. They used guerrilla warfare tactics to ambush the Seleucids, catching them off guard and forcing them to retreat in confusion.

The Seleucids fought hard, but the Maccabees were able to hold their ground and push them back. Eventually, the Seleucids were defeated and forced to retreat. The Maccabees had won a decisive victory and secured the mountain pass, allowing them to continue their rebellion against the Seleucid Empire.

After the battle, Judas and his troops celebrated their victory. They had not only defeated the Seleucids but also proved that they were a force to be reckoned with. The Maccabees were now one step closer to achieving their goal of freedom for their people.

As for Seron, the Seleucid commander, it was said that he was killed in the battle. Though, some historians believe that he was only defeated and not killed. Regardless, the Maccabees had dealt a significant blow to the Seleucid Empire and gained the upper hand in the rebellion.

The Battle of Beth Horon was a pivotal moment in the Maccabean Revolt. It marked a turning point in the rebellion and set the stage for further victories and ultimately the independence of the Hasmonean kingdom. The Maccabees had shown their bravery and determination in the face of overwhelming odds and had secured a place in the annals of history.

CHAPTER 8 Battle of Emmaus

Image 17 https://historycollection.com/at-the-battle-of-emmaus-maccabee-used-guerrilla-tactics-to-destroy-the-seleucid-army/3/

The Battle of Emmaus occurred around September 165 BC, during the Maccabean Revolt. The Maccabean Revolt was a rebellion against the Seleucid Empire, led by the Jewish leader Judas Maccabeus, also known as Judah Maccabee. The Seleucid Empire was led by generals Gorgias, Ptolemy the son of Dorymenes, and Nicanor. The battle took place near Emmaus, a location that is not specified in the historical accounts.

The Maccabee rebels, led by Judas Maccabeus, emerged victorious in the battle. They were able to achieve this by utilizing a tactic of marching by night and surprising the Seleucid camp while many of the soldiers were absent. The Maccabees were able to loot the Greek camp for valuables, which would have been useful in helping to fund their rebellion. They also likely acquired weapons, which would have helped them in their future battles.

The Maccabean Revolt was a significant event in Jewish history, as it was a rebellion against a powerful empire and the Maccabees were able to achieve a series of victories against the Seleucid Empire. The Battle of Emmaus was one of these victories, which helped to further the cause of the Maccabees in their fight for independence.

Primary Sources

The Battle of Emmaus is recorded in several primary sources, including the books of 1 Maccabees (1 Maccabees 3:38–4:25), 2 Maccabees (2 Maccabees 8:8–8:36, and Josephus's Antiquities of the Jews Book 12. These primary sources provide historical accounts of the battle, each with its own perspective and level of detail.

1 Maccabees provides a more detailed description of the battle and the rebel army, and it is believed that the author may have even been a personal eyewitness to the battle. 2 Maccabees, on the other hand, gives a more accurate depiction of the Seleucid forces and commanders. However, its account of the battle is more focused on moral lessons and emphasizing the righteousness of Judas Maccabeus and the Maccabee cause.

Josephus's Antiquities of the Jews Book 12 also includes an account of the battle, which may provide additional information and insights. It is important to consider all primary sources and to evaluate them critically, in order to gain a more complete understanding of the historical event.

1 Maccabees 3:38-4:25 New Revised Standard Version, Anglicised Catholic Edition

Preparations for Battle

[38] Lysias chose Ptolemy son of Dorymenes, and Nicanor and Gorgias, able men among the Friends of the king, [39] and sent with them forty thousand infantry and seven thousand cavalry to go into the land of Judah and destroy it, as the king had commanded. [40] So they set out with their entire force, and when they arrived they encamped near Emmaus in the plain. [41] When the traders of the region heard what was said to them, they took silver and gold in immense amounts, and fetters, and went to the camp to get the Israelites for slaves. And forces from Syria and the land of the Philistines joined with them.

[42] Now Judas and his brothers saw that misfortunes had increased and that the forces were encamped in their territory. They also learned what the king had commanded to be done to the people to cause their

final destruction. ⁴³ But they said to one another, 'Let us restore the ruins of our people, and fight for our people and the sanctuary.' ⁴⁴ So the congregation assembled to be ready for battle, and to pray and ask for mercy and compassion.

⁴⁵ Jerusalem was uninhabited like a wilderness;
    not one of her children went in or out.
The sanctuary was trampled down,
    and aliens held the citadel;
    it was a lodging-place for the Gentiles.
Joy was taken from Jacob;
    the flute and the harp ceased to play.

⁴⁶ Then they gathered together and went to Mizpah, opposite Jerusalem, because Israel formerly had a place of prayer in Mizpah. ⁴⁷ They fasted that day, put on sackcloth and sprinkled ashes on their heads, and tore their clothes. ⁴⁸ And they opened the book of the law to inquire into those matters about which the Gentiles consulted the images of their gods. ⁴⁹ They also brought the vestments of the priesthood and the first fruits and the tithes, and they stirred up the nazirites who had completed their days; ⁵⁰ and they cried aloud to Heaven, saying,

'What shall we do with these?
    Where shall we take them?
⁵¹ Your sanctuary is trampled down and profaned,
    and your priests mourn in humiliation.
⁵² Here the Gentiles are assembled against us to destroy us;
    you know what they plot against us.
⁵³ How will we be able to withstand them,
    if you do not help us?'

⁵⁴ Then they sounded the trumpets and gave a loud shout. ⁵⁵ After this Judas appointed leaders of the people, in charge of thousands and hundreds and fifties and tens. ⁵⁶ Those who were building houses, or were about to be married, or were planting a vineyard, or were faint-hearted, he told to go home again, in accordance with the law. ⁵⁷ Then the army marched out and encamped to the south of Emmaus.

[58] And Judas said, 'Arm yourselves and be courageous. Be ready early in the morning to fight with these Gentiles who have assembled against us to destroy us and our sanctuary. [59] It is better for us to die in battle than to see the misfortunes of our nation and of the sanctuary. [60] But as his will in heaven may be, so shall he do.'

The Battle at Emmaus

4 Now Gorgias took five thousand infantry and one thousand picked cavalry, and this division moved out by night [2] to fall upon the camp of the Jews and attack them suddenly. Men from the citadel were his guides. [3] But Judas heard of it, and he and his warriors moved out to attack the king's force in Emmaus [4] while the division was still absent from the camp. [5] When Gorgias entered the camp of Judas by night, he found no one there, so he looked for them in the hills, because he said, 'These men are running away from us.'

[6] At daybreak Judas appeared in the plain with three thousand men, but they did not have armour and swords such as they desired. [7] And they saw the camp of the Gentiles, strong and fortified, with cavalry all around it; and these men were trained in war. [8] But Judas said to those who were with him, 'Do not fear their numbers or be afraid when they charge. [9] Remember how our ancestors were saved at the Red Sea, when Pharaoh with his forces pursued them. [10] And now, let us cry to Heaven, to see whether he will favour us and remember his covenant with our ancestors and crush this army before us today. [11] Then all the Gentiles will know that there is one who redeems and saves Israel.'

[12] When the foreigners looked up and saw them coming against them, [13] they went out from their camp to battle. Then the men with Judas blew their trumpets [14] and engaged in battle. The Gentiles were crushed, and fled into the plain, [15] and all those in the rear fell by the sword. They pursued them to Gazara, and to the plains of Idumea, and to Azotus and Jamnia; and three thousand of them fell. [16] Then Judas and his force turned back from pursuing them, [17] and he said to the people, 'Do not be greedy for plunder, for there is a battle before us; [18] Gorgias and his force are near us in the hills. But stand now

against our enemies and fight them, and afterwards seize the plunder boldly.'

[19] Just as Judas was finishing this speech, a detachment appeared, coming out of the hills. [20] They saw that their army had been put to flight, and that the Jews were burning the camp, for the smoke that was seen showed what had happened. [21] When they perceived this, they were greatly frightened, and when they also saw the army of Judas drawn up in the plain for battle, [22] they all fled into the land of the Philistines. [23] Then Judas returned to plunder the camp, and they seized a great amount of gold and silver, and cloth dyed blue and sea purple, and great riches. [24] On their return they sang hymns and praises to Heaven—'For he is good, for his mercy endures for ever.' [25] Thus Israel had a great deliverance that day.

2 Maccabees 8:8-36 New Revised Standard Version, Anglicised Catholic Edition

[8] When Philip saw that the man was gaining ground little by little, and that he was pushing ahead with more frequent successes, he wrote to Ptolemy, the governor of Coelesyria and Phoenicia, to come to the aid of the king's government. [9] Then Ptolemy promptly appointed Nicanor son of Patroclus, one of the king's chief Friends, and sent him, in command of no fewer than twenty thousand Gentiles of all nations, to wipe out the whole race of Judea. He associated with him Gorgias, a general and a man of experience in military service. [10] Nicanor determined to make up for the king the tribute due to the Romans, two thousand talents, by selling the captured Jews into slavery. [11] So he immediately sent to the towns on the sea coast, inviting them to buy Jewish slaves and promising to hand over ninety slaves for a talent, not expecting the judgement from the Almighty that was about to overtake him.

Preparation for Battle

[12] Word came to Judas concerning Nicanor's invasion; and when he told his companions of the arrival of the army, [13] those who were cowardly and distrustful of God's justice ran off and got away. [14] Others sold all their remaining property, and at the same time implored the Lord to rescue those who had been sold by the ungodly

Nicanor before he ever met them, [15] if not for their own sake, then for the sake of the covenants made with their ancestors, and because he had called them by his holy and glorious name. [16] But Maccabeus gathered his forces together, to the number of six thousand, and exhorted them not to be frightened by the enemy and not to fear the great multitude of Gentiles who were wickedly coming against them, but to fight nobly, [17] keeping before their eyes the lawless outrage that the Gentiles had committed against the holy place, and the torture of the derided city, and besides, the overthrow of their ancestral way of life. [18] 'For they trust to arms and acts of daring', he said, 'but we trust in the Almighty God, who is able with a single nod to strike down those who are coming against us, and even, if necessary, the whole world.'

[19] Moreover, he told them of the occasions when help came to their ancestors; how, in the time of Sennacherib, when one hundred and eighty-five thousand perished, [20] and the time of the battle against the Galatians that took place in Babylonia, when eight thousand Jews fought along with four thousand Macedonians; yet when the Macedonians were hard pressed, the eight thousand, by the help that came to them from heaven, destroyed one hundred and twenty thousand Galatians and took a great amount of booty.

Judas Defeats Nicanor

[21] With these words he filled them with courage and made them ready to die for their laws and their country; then he divided his army into four parts. [22] He appointed his brothers also, Simon and Joseph and Jonathan, each to command a division, putting fifteen hundred men under each. [23] Besides, he appointed Eleazar to read aloud from the holy book, and gave the watchword, 'The help of God'; then, leading the first division himself, he joined battle with Nicanor.

[24] With the Almighty as their ally, they killed more than nine thousand of the enemy, and wounded and disabled most of Nicanor's army, and forced them all to flee. [25] They captured the money of those who had come to buy them as slaves. After pursuing them for some distance, they were obliged to return because the hour was late. [26] It was the day before the sabbath, and for that reason they did not

continue their pursuit. [27] When they had collected the arms of the enemy and stripped them of their spoils, they kept the sabbath, giving great praise and thanks to the Lord, who had preserved them for that day and allotted it to them as the beginning of mercy. [28] After the sabbath they gave some of the spoils to those who had been tortured and to the widows and orphans, and distributed the rest among themselves and their children. [29] When they had done this, they made common supplication and implored the merciful Lord to be wholly reconciled with his servants.

Judas Defeats Timothy and Bacchides

[30] In encounters with the forces of Timothy and Bacchides they killed more than twenty thousand of them and got possession of some exceedingly high strongholds, and they divided a very large amount of plunder, giving to those who had been tortured and to the orphans and widows, and also to the aged, shares equal to their own. [31] They collected the arms of the enemy, and carefully stored all of them in strategic places; the rest of the spoils they carried to Jerusalem. [32] They killed the commander of Timothy's forces, a most wicked man, and one who had greatly troubled the Jews. [33] While they were celebrating the victory in the city of their ancestors, they burned those who had set fire to the sacred gates, Callisthenes and some others, who had fled into one little house; so these received the proper reward for their impiety.

[34] The thrice-accursed Nicanor, who had brought the thousand merchants to buy the Jews, [35] having been humbled with the help of the Lord by opponents whom he regarded as of the least account, took off his splendid uniform and made his way alone like a runaway slave across the country until he reached Antioch, having succeeded chiefly in the destruction of his own army! [36] So he who had undertaken to secure tribute for the Romans by the capture of the people of Jerusalem proclaimed that the Jews had a Defender, and that therefore the Jews were invulnerable, because they followed the laws ordained by him.

Background

The background to the Battle of Emmaus, which took place around September 165 BC, is rooted in the actions of King Antiochus IV Epiphanes of the Seleucid Empire. Antiochus had gathered an army from the western part of his empire with the intention of leaving for an expedition to the eastern satrapies in Babylonia and Persia. His goals were to replace or do battle with rebellious governors, deter the growing Parthian Empire from invading, and restore a flow of taxes to the capital.

In order to do this, Antiochus left Lysias as regent in the Seleucid capital Antioch and to raise his young son, the future Antiochus V. At the time, Jerusalem was still ruled by Seleucid-friendly Hellenist Jews and High Priest Menelaus. Lysias, at the request of Menelaus, dispatched a force, led by Ptolemy son of Dorymenes, to aid the ruling faction of Hellenist Jews and defeat the countryside rebels led by Judas Maccabeus. Ptolemy was accompanied by Gorgias and Nicanor as commanders.

2 Maccabees suggests that Nicanor, one of the Seleucid generals, intended to raise money by using the army to enslave Jews and then sell them to pay off a 2,000-talent debt the Seleucids owed to the Roman Republic. This highlights the larger political and economic motivations behind the Seleucid actions and the Maccabean Revolt, as well as the complex dynamics at play in the region at the time.

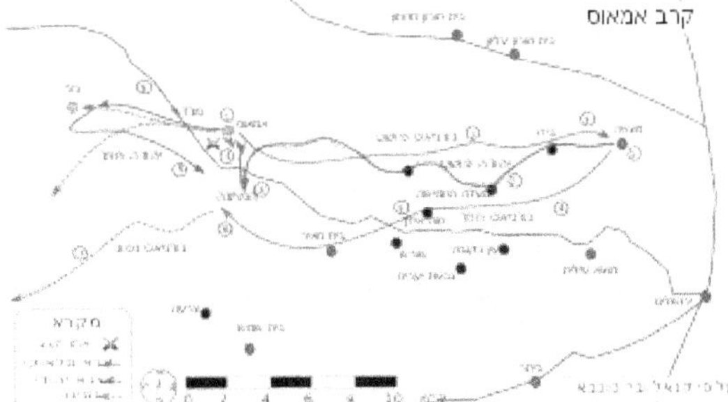

Image 18 Troop movements during the Battle of Emmaus. Blue arrows shows a hypothesized line of the Maccabees march from Mizpah to the west, red arrows shows proposed movement of Gorgias's raiding force; dotted red lines are the direction of the Seleucid camp's retreat.

Battle

The Battle of Emmaus took place around September 165 BC during the Maccabean Revolt between Judean rebels, led by Judas Maccabeus (Judah Maccabee), and an expedition of Seleucid Empire forces under generals Gorgias, Ptolemy the son of Dorymenes, and Nicanor. The Seleucids had established their base camp at the town of Emmaus, which is located at the eastern edge of the Ayalon Valley and along the western border of Judea. Emmaus was an excellent location for a base camp as it had easy access to numerous routes into the Judean hills and good water. Emmaus was also largely flat, which allowed the use of cavalry and denied any advantages to the rebel forces from hilly terrain.

Judas Maccabeus's camp was located in the town of Mizpah, north of Jerusalem. Gorgias planned to attack Judas's concentration of troops after receiving word of them, possibly through intentional leaks by Judas himself. Judas's scouts and spies found out that Gorgias was leading troops on a march against his camp and was planning to surprise the Jewish rebels in a night-time attack.

Judas then abandoned his camp at Mizpah and led his forces to Emmaus, to attack the expedition base camp that remained there. Using a small force of about 3,000 soldiers, Judas's troops were able to surprise the Seleucid camp at Emmaus at dawn and forced the unprepared Seleucid soldiers to retreat to the southwest, toward Idumea. Gorgias returned to Emmaus, only to find his camp destroyed. The Maccabees looted the camp, taking gold and silver, and likely also took abandoned Seleucid weapons.

The outcome of the battle was quite influential. The Maccabees had previously defeated small detachments of Seleucid troops in earlier clashes against Apollonius and Seron, but with this victory, the Maccabees proved that they could challenge larger numbers of Seleucid troops and could make complicated plans and tactical ploys. This helped set the stage for the eventual independence of the Hasmonean kingdom.

Analysis

The primary source 1 Maccabees is considered to be generally reliable in its depiction of the Battle of Emmaus. However, some scholars have questioned the accuracy of certain aspects of the portrayal of the battle. It is common in accounts of battles during the

Maccabean Revolt for the rebels and authors of 1 and 2 Maccabees to exaggerate the size of the Seleucid forces. This was likely done to create more impressive morale-raising stories.

The book of 1 Maccabees claims that Gorgias's force that split from the camp consisted of 5,000 soldiers, 1,000 cavalrymen, and allied Hellenist Jews from the Acra as guides. This would be an unwieldy number for a surprise attack that would travel through the narrow Beth Horon ascent, and the Seleucids had perhaps only 5,000 cavalry in the entire Western half of their empire. Some later manuscripts of 1 Maccabees adds that the rebel troops lacked "helmets and slings and stones and armor" as well in the battle; this is considered likely to be a gloss of an unknown scribe copying the material, and unlikely to be historical. The reported Seleucid casualty numbers are also considered implausibly high: 3,000 defeated according to 1 Maccabees, and 9,000 according to 2 Maccabees.

Judas's speeches and prayers in the book of 1 Maccabees are also seen as compositions of the historian and not actual transcriptions. They are written in the style of Hellenistic historians to make them more literary. In the case of the Battle of Emmaus, Judas's speech in 1 Maccabees does not make sense in context as it is given just before the rebels attack the base camp. This is unlikely as during a surprise attack, every minute of delay after being spotted gives the defenders more time to prepare. It is more likely that any speeches or special instructions were given during the ceremony held at Mizpah, a day earlier.

Fictional Story of the Battle of Emmaus

Once upon a time, in the land of Judea, a great rebellion was taking place. The Jewish people, led by a brave warrior named Judas Maccabeus, were fighting against the powerful Seleucid Empire for their freedom and independence. The Seleucid king, Antiochus IV Epiphanes, had left for an expedition to the eastern satrapies in Babylonia and Persia, leaving Lysias in charge as regent in the Seleucid capital Antioch.

Lysias, at the request of Menelaus, the Seleucid-friendly High Priest of Jerusalem, dispatched a force led by Ptolemy the son of Dorymenes, Gorgias, and Nicanor to defeat the Jewish rebels and aid the ruling faction of Hellenist Jews. The Seleucid forces established their base camp at the town of Emmaus, which was an excellent spot to project power from with easy access to numerous routes into the Judean hills and good water.

Judas Maccabeus, however, was not one to be easily defeated. He and his army were camped in the town of Mizpah, north of Jerusalem. Gorgias planned to attack Judas's concentration of troops after receiving word of them. But Judas, being the clever warrior he was, ensured that word of his location would leak by performing obvious ceremonies and rituals.

Judas's scouts and spies found out that Gorgias was leading troops on a march against his camp and was planning to surprise the Jewish rebels in a night-time attack. Judas, knowing that Gorgias's forces were unprepared for a night battle, led his own army to Emmaus, where they attacked the Seleucid camp at dawn. The Seleucid forces, surprised and unprepared, were forced to retreat and the Maccabees looted the camp, taking gold and silver, and likely weapons to help further their cause.

The Battle of Emmaus was a turning point in the rebellion. The Maccabees proved that they could challenge larger numbers of Seleucid troops, and could make complicated plans and tactical ploys. They had defeated the Seleucids in a decisive victory and the morale of the Jewish people was at an all-time high. The Seleucids, realizing they were no match for the Maccabees, retreated to the coastal plains and the Maccabees were able to claim Emmaus as their own.

The Battle of Emmaus was just the beginning of the Maccabean Revolt, but it served as a powerful symbol of hope and strength for the Jewish people. They had shown that they were not to be underestimated, and that they were willing to fight for their freedom and independence. Judas Maccabeus and his army continued to fight for the cause, and eventually, they were able to secure their freedom and establish the Hasmonean kingdom.

The Battle of Emmaus will forever be remembered as a pivotal moment in Jewish history, where a small group of rebels, led by a brave and cunning leader, were able to defeat a powerful empire and claim their independence. It serves as a reminder that even the smallest and seemingly weakest among us have the power to make a difference and change the course of history.

CHAPTER 9 Battle of Beth Zu

Image 19 The Ruins of Beth Zur, early 20th century

The Battle of Beth Zur was a military engagement that took place in October 164 BC between the Maccabees, a group of Jewish rebels led by Judas Maccabeus, and the Seleucid Greek army led by Regent Lysias. The battle was fought at the location of Beth Zur, a town located in the western part of Judea. According to the primary sources, such as the books of Maccabees, the Maccabees emerged victorious in the battle. However, the true significance of this victory is debated among historians. Some suggest that the battle's outcome was inconclusive, and the Maccabees' victory may have been the result of good luck.

After the battle, the Seleucid army and Lysias decided to return to the capital instead of continuing their campaign. This was likely due to the news of Seleucid King Antiochus IV Epiphanes' death, which reached Judea in the days following the battle. The leadership transition in the Seleucid Empire required Lysias and his army to return to the capital to handle the political situation. This gave the Maccabees an opportunity to capture Jerusalem, which they were able to do soon after.

The Battle of Beth Zur was a key moment in the Maccabean Revolt, a conflict fought between the Maccabees, a group of Jewish rebels, and the Seleucid Greek army. The Maccabees, led by Judas Maccabeus, were fighting for Jewish independence and religious freedom. The Seleucids, led by Regent Lysias, were fighting to maintain control over Judea. The battle was fought at Beth Zur, a fortification in the Judean hills, in October 164 BC. According to the books of Maccabees, the Maccabees emerged victorious. However, the true outcome of the battle is uncertain and some scholars believe that it was inconclusive. Nevertheless, the Maccabees were able to take advantage of the situation after the battle as the news of the death of Seleucid King Antiochus IV Epiphanes reached Judea, Lysias and his army returned to the capital to handle the leadership transition and the Maccabees were able to capture Jerusalem soon after. This victory was crucial in the Maccabean Revolt, as it marked the Maccabees as a powerful force and helped pave the way for the eventual independence of the Hasmonean kingdom.

Primary Sources

The Battle of Beth Zur is a key historical event recorded in primary sources such as the books of 1 Maccabees (1 Maccabees 4:26–35), 2 Maccabees (2 Maccabees 11:1–15), and Josephus's Antiquities of the Jews. These sources provide different perspectives on the timing of the battle, with 1 Maccabees stating that it occurred before the capture of Jerusalem and the purification of the Temple, while 2 Maccabees suggests that it happened after these events. Scholars have debated which account is more accurate, with many historians preferring the version in 1 Maccabees as it was written closer to the events and the author was possibly an eyewitness. However, Josephus's account largely echoes 1 Maccabees, with the addition that the Maccabees clashed with only the advance troops of the Seleucids, which is considered a plausible addition. The outcome of the battle is also uncertain and disputed, with some scholars believe that it may have been inconclusive.

1 Maccabees 4:26-35 New Revised Standard Version, Anglicised Catholic Edition

First Campaign of Lysias

[26] Those of the foreigners who escaped went and reported to Lysias all that had happened. [27] When he heard it, he was perplexed and discouraged, for things had not happened to Israel as he had intended, nor had they turned out as the king had ordered. [28] But the next year he mustered sixty thousand picked infantry and five thousand cavalry to subdue them. [29] They came into Idumea and encamped at Beth-zur, and Judas met them with ten thousand men.

[30] When he saw that their army was strong, he prayed, saying, 'Blessed are you, O Saviour of Israel, who crushed the attack of the mighty warrior by the hand of your servant David, and gave the camp of the Philistines into the hands of Jonathan son of Saul, and of the man who carried his armour. [31] Hem in this army by the hand of your people Israel, and let them be ashamed of their troops and their cavalry. [32] Fill them with cowardice; melt the boldness of their strength; let them tremble in their destruction. [33] Strike them down with the sword of those who love you, and let all who know your name praise you with hymns.'

[34] Then both sides attacked, and there fell of the army of Lysias five thousand men; they fell in action. [35] When Lysias saw the rout of his troops and observed the boldness that inspired those of Judas, and how ready they were either to live or to die nobly, he withdrew to Antioch and enlisted mercenaries in order to invade Judea again with an even larger army.

2 Maccabees 11:1-15 New Revised Standard Version, Anglicised Catholic Edition

Lysias Besieges Beth-zur

11 Very soon after this, Lysias, the king's guardian and kinsman, who was in charge of the government, being vexed at what had happened, [2] gathered about eighty thousand infantry and all his cavalry and came against the Jews. He intended to make the city a home for Greeks, [3] and to levy tribute on the temple as he did on the sacred places of the other nations, and to put the high-priesthood up for sale every year. [4] He took no account whatever of the power of God, but was elated with his tens of thousands of infantry, and his thousands of cavalry, and his eighty elephants. [5] Invading Judea, he approached Beth-zur, which was a fortified place about five stadia from Jerusalem, and pressed it hard.

[6] When Maccabeus and his men got word that Lysias was besieging the strongholds, they and all the people, with lamentations and tears, prayed the Lord to send a good angel to save Israel. [7] Maccabeus himself was the first to take up arms, and he urged the others to risk their lives with him to aid their kindred. Then they eagerly rushed off together. [8] And there, while they were still near Jerusalem, a horseman appeared at their head, clothed in white and brandishing weapons of gold. [9] And together they all praised the merciful God, and were strengthened in heart, ready to assail not only humans but the wildest animals or walls of iron. [10] They advanced in battle order, having their heavenly ally, for the Lord had mercy on them. [11] They hurled themselves like lions against the enemy, and laid low eleven thousand of them and sixteen hundred cavalry, and forced all the rest to flee. [12] Most of them got away stripped and wounded, and Lysias himself escaped by disgraceful flight.

Lysias Makes Peace with the Jews

[13] As he was not without intelligence, he pondered over the defeat that had befallen him, and realized that the Hebrews were invincible because the mighty God fought on their side. So he sent to them [14] and persuaded them to settle everything on just terms, promising that he would persuade the king, constraining him to be their friend. [15] Maccabeus, having regard for the common good, agreed to all that Lysias urged. For the king granted every request in behalf of the Jews which Maccabeus delivered to Lysias in writing.

Background

The background of the Battle of Beth Zur took place in the context of the Maccabean Revolt, a rebellion of the Jewish people against the Seleucid Empire, led by Judas Maccabeus (Judah Maccabee) and his brothers. The Seleucid King Antiochus IV Epiphanes had left for an expedition to the eastern satrapies in Babylonia and Persia, leaving his regent Lysias in charge of the empire's western half. The Maccabees had already won a significant victory against the Seleucids in the Battle of Emmaus, which took place in 165 BC. However, Lysias attempted to negotiate with the rebels for several months in an attempt to restore order in the Judean countryside. When these negotiations failed, Lysias marshaled an army and camped at Beth Zur, a fortified place near Jerusalem, in preparation for a battle against the Maccabees. The exact timing and details of the events leading up to the Battle of Beth Zur are debated among scholars, with different accounts provided in primary sources such as the books of Maccabees and Josephus's Antiquities of the Jews.

The timing of the Battle of Beth Zur is also a point of debate among historians. According to 1 Maccabees, Lysias initiated an expedition, was defeated at Beth Zur, Jerusalem was taken, and the Second Temple was cleansed. 2 Maccabees, on the other hand, indicates that Lysias's expedition and the Battle of Beth Zur happened after the taking of Jerusalem and the purification of the Temple. This has led some scholars to believe that Lysias only made a single expedition to Judea, rather than the account in 1 Maccabees of two expeditions separated by two years.

In any case, the Maccabees' victory at Beth Zur was a crucial moment in the Maccabean Revolt. It solidified their control over Jerusalem and set the stage for the establishment of the Hasmonean kingdom. Additionally, the fact that Lysias was forced to negotiate with the Maccabees and that he eventually retreated, showed the Maccabees' strength and the weakness of the Seleucid Empire in the region.

Battle

The Maccabees, led by Judas Maccabeus, were outnumbered and outmatched by the Seleucid army led by Regent Lysias. However, they were able to use their knowledge of the terrain and their guerrilla tactics to their advantage. They attacked the Seleucid camp at Beth Zur with swift, surprise raids, causing confusion and chaos among the enemy ranks. The Seleucids, caught off guard, were unable to effectively respond to the Maccabees' relentless attacks.

Despite the Maccabees' initial success, Lysias was able to regroup and rally his troops. He ordered a counterattack, but the Maccabees, knowing they could not defeat the Seleucids in a full-scale battle, retreated into the hills. Lysias, not wanting to risk losing more men in pursuit, decided to retreat back to his main force and regroup.

The Maccabees, on the other hand, were able to use their victory to bolster morale and gain support among the Jewish population. News of the battle spread quickly, and many Jews who had previously been hesitant to join the rebellion were now willing to fight for their freedom. The Maccabees were also able to capture weapons and other valuable resources from the Seleucid camp, which they would later use in future battles.

In the end, the Battle of Beth Zur was a significant victory for the Maccabees, although the Seleucids still held the upper hand in terms of military might. However, the Maccabees' success in this battle would pave the way for future victories and ultimately lead to the establishment of the Hasmonean Kingdom.

Aftermath

The aftermath of the Battle of Beth Zur was significant for both the Maccabees and the Seleucids. According to the First Book of Maccabees, the Maccabees emerged victorious from the battle, which convinced Lysias to return to Antioch to replenish his forces after sustaining heavy casualties. However, this account is somewhat distrusted by some historians as fitting the narrative that the pro-

Hasmonean source would want to tell. Some scholars believe that the battle was inconclusive based on the description given.

Regardless of the outcome of the battle, Lysias was unable to continue his campaign due to the death of Antiochus IV. He had to withdraw and cede the field to the Maccabees, as his main priority was to be in the capital Antioch with as many military units loyal to him as possible to stave off any succession challenges to the new boy king Antiochus V Eupator, who was only 9 years old.

On the other hand, the Maccabees may have intentionally declined to attempt to conquer Jerusalem earlier, in the knowledge that doing so would have provoked a fierce response from Antiochus IV. The resulting succession struggle enabled the Maccabees time to establish new "facts on the ground" by taking Jerusalem, cleansing the Temple, and making clear they were in control of Judea, although they did not challenge the Acra immediately with its garrison of Greeks and Hellenist-friendly Jews.

Analysis

It is likely that the Battle of Beth Zur was a relatively small engagement between the Maccabees and Seleucids, with both sides withdrawing in good order after the clash. The significance of the battle lies in the fact that it occurred at a time when Lysias, the Seleucid regent, was forced to withdraw and return to Antioch due to the death of King Antiochus IV Epiphanes and the need to secure the succession of the new king, Antiochus V Eupator. This withdrawal allowed the Maccabees to establish control over Jerusalem and the surrounding areas, leading to the eventual independence of the Hasmonean kingdom. While the primary sources of 1 Maccabees and 2 Maccabees provide accounts of the battle, the figures of the size of the Seleucid army and the casualties are likely exaggerated for the purpose of morale-boosting and to enhance the image of the Maccabees as heroic fighters.

Fictional Story of the Battle of Beth Zur

Once upon a time, in the ancient land of Judea, a fierce battle was fought at the fortress of Beth Zur. The Roman army, led by the ruthless General Marcus, had been sent to crush the rebellion of the Jewish people, who had risen up against their oppressors.

Beth Zur, perched on a rocky hilltop, was the key to controlling the region, and the Roman army had set its sights on the fortress. The Jewish defenders, led by the brave and determined Judas Maccabeus, were determined to protect their homeland and their people.

The battle began at dawn, with the Romans launching a fierce assault on the fortress. Arrows flew through the air, and the sound of clashing swords filled the air. The Jewish defenders fought bravely, but they were outnumbered and outmatched.

Despite the odds against them, the defenders of Beth Zur refused to give up. They launched counterattacks and used their knowledge of the terrain to their advantage. They fought with all their might, determined to protect their people and their land.

For hours the battle raged on, with neither side gaining the upper hand. But as the sun began to set, the tide of the battle began to turn. The Roman army, weary from the long and bloody fight, began to falter.

Taking advantage of this, Judas Maccabeus rallied his men and launched a final, desperate charge. The defenders of Beth Zur fought with all their might, their hearts filled with the courage and determination of their people.

In the end, the Roman army was defeated and the fortress of Beth Zur was saved. The Jewish people had won a great victory, and they celebrated the bravery and sacrifice of their heroes. The fortress of Beth Zur remained a symbol of their freedom and determination, and the memory of the battle lived on for generations to come.

Edward D. Andrews

CHAPTER 10 Maccabee Campaigns of 163 BC

The Maccabean Revolt was a series of campaigns fought by the Maccabee rebels against the Seleucid Empire in 163 BC. The rebels fought multiple enemies, including Seleucid garrisons, hired mercenaries, and hostile non-Jewish inhabitants in regions such as Ammon, Gilead, Galilee, Idumea, and Judea's coastal plain. The main Seleucid armies were elsewhere at the time, allowing the Maccabees to expand their influence. The Maccabees did not hold territory, but engaged in raids and retributive attacks. The book 1 Maccabees describes a vicious campaign of extermination on both sides, with the Maccabees massacring Gentiles they believed were involved and burning down their towns. The Maccabees also invited Jewish refugees back to Judea and escorted them under the safety of their army.

Primary Sources

The campaigns against Timothy, a Greek individual, and the local non-Jewish population, commonly referred to as Gentiles, are documented in various primary sources. These sources include the books of 1 Maccabees (1 Maccabees 5), 2 Maccabees (2 Maccabees 10:14–38, 2 Maccabees 12:10–37), and Josephus's Antiquities of the Jews Book 12, Chapter 8. It is worth noting that 2 Maccabees also briefly mentions Timothy and his armies in relation to the Battle of Emmaus (2 Maccabees 8:30–8:33), although it is generally assumed by historians that this reference is a "flash-forward" in time to describe Timothy's eventual defeat rather than an actual occurrence during the Emmaus campaign of 164 BC.

1 Maccabees 5 New Revised Standard Version, Anglicised Catholic Edition

Wars with Neighbouring Peoples

5 When the Gentiles all around heard that the altar had been rebuilt and the sanctuary dedicated as it was before, they became very angry, [2] and they determined to destroy the descendants of Jacob who lived among them. So they began to kill and destroy among the people. [3] But Judas made war on the descendants of Esau in Idumea, at Akrabattene, because they kept lying in wait for Israel. He dealt them a heavy blow and humbled them and despoiled them. [4] He also remembered the wickedness of the sons of Baean, who were a trap and a snare to the people and ambushed them on the highways. [5] They were shut up by him in their towers; and he encamped against them, vowed their complete destruction, and burned with fire their towers and all who were in them. [6] Then he crossed over to attack the Ammonites, where he found a strong band and many people, with Timothy as their leader. [7] He engaged in many battles with them, and they were crushed before him; he struck them down. [8] He also took Jazer and its villages; then he returned to Judea.

Liberation of Galilean Jews

[9] Now the Gentiles in Gilead gathered together against the Israelites who lived in their territory, and planned to destroy them. But

they fled to the stronghold of Dathema, [10] and sent to Judas and his brothers a letter that said, 'The Gentiles around us have gathered together to destroy us. [11] They are preparing to come and capture the stronghold to which we have fled, and Timothy is leading their forces. [12] Now then, come and rescue us from their hands, for many of us have fallen, [13] and all our kindred who were in the land of Tob have been killed; the enemy have captured their wives and children and goods, and have destroyed about a thousand people there.'

[14] While the letter was still being read, other messengers, with their garments torn, came from Galilee and made a similar report; [15] they said that the people of Ptolemais and Tyre and Sidon, and all Galilee of the Gentiles, had gathered together against them 'to annihilate us.' [16] When Judas and the people heard these messages, a great assembly was called to determine what they should do for their kindred who were in distress and were being attacked by enemies. [17] Then Judas said to his brother Simon, 'Choose your men and go and rescue your kindred in Galilee; Jonathan my brother and I will go to Gilead.' [18] But he left Joseph, son of Zechariah, and Azariah, a leader of the people, with the rest of the forces, in Judea to guard it; [19] and he gave them this command, 'Take charge of this people, but do not engage in battle with the Gentiles until we return.' [20] Then three thousand men were assigned to Simon to go to Galilee, and eight thousand to Judas for Gilead.

[21] So Simon went to Galilee and fought many battles against the Gentiles, and the Gentiles were crushed before him. [22] He pursued them to the gate of Ptolemais; as many as three thousand of the Gentiles fell, and he despoiled them. [23] Then he took the Jews of Galilee and Arbatta, with their wives and children, and all they possessed, and led them to Judea with great rejoicing.

Judas and Jonathan in Gilead

[24] Judas Maccabeus and his brother Jonathan crossed the Jordan and made three days' journey into the wilderness. [25] They encountered the Nabateans, who met them peaceably and told them all that had happened to their kindred in Gilead: [26] 'Many of them have been shut up in Bozrah and Bosor, in Alema and Chaspho, Maked and

Carnaim'—all these towns were strong and large— ²⁷'and some have been shut up in the other towns of Gilead; the enemy are getting ready to attack the strongholds tomorrow and capture and destroy all these people in a single day.'

²⁸Then Judas and his army quickly turned back by the wilderness road to Bozrah; and he took the town, and killed every male by the edge of the sword; then he seized all its spoils and burned it with fire. ²⁹He left the place at night, and they went all the way to the stronghold of Dathema. ³⁰At dawn they looked out and saw a large company, which could not be counted, carrying ladders and engines of war to capture the stronghold, and attacking the Jews within. ³¹So Judas saw that the battle had begun and that the cry of the town went up to Heaven, with trumpets and loud shouts, ³²and he said to the men of his forces, 'Fight today for your kindred!' ³³Then he came up behind them in three companies, who sounded their trumpets and cried aloud in prayer. ³⁴And when the army of Timothy realized that it was Maccabeus, they fled before him, and he dealt them a heavy blow. As many as eight thousand of them fell that day.

³⁵Next he turned aside to Maapha, and fought against it and took it; and he killed every male in it, plundered it, and burned it with fire. ³⁶From there he marched on and took Chaspho, Maked, and Bosor, and the other towns of Gilead.

³⁷After these things Timothy gathered another army and encamped opposite Raphon, on the other side of the stream. ³⁸Judas sent men to spy out the camp, and they reported to him, 'All the Gentiles around us have gathered to him; it is a very large force. ³⁹They also have hired Arabs to help them, and they are encamped across the stream, ready to come and fight against you.' And Judas went to meet them.

⁴⁰Now as Judas and his army drew near to the stream of water, Timothy said to the officers of his forces, 'If he crosses over to us first, we will not be able to resist him, for he will surely defeat us. ⁴¹But if he shows fear and camps on the other side of the river, we will cross over to him and defeat him.' ⁴²When Judas approached the stream of water, he stationed the officers of the army at the stream and gave

them this command, 'Permit no one to encamp, but make them all enter the battle.' [43] Then he crossed over against them first, and the whole army followed him. All the Gentiles were defeated before him, and they threw away their arms and fled into the sacred precincts at Carnaim. [44] But he took the town and burned the sacred precincts with fire, together with all who were in them. Thus Carnaim was conquered; they could stand before Judas no longer.

The Return to Jerusalem

[45] Then Judas gathered together all the Israelites in Gilead, the small and the great, with their wives and children and goods, a very large company, to go to the land of Judah. [46] So they came to Ephron. This was a large and very strong town on the road, and they could not go around it to the right or to the left; they had to go through it. [47] But the people of the town shut them out and blocked up the gates with stones.

[48] Judas sent them this friendly message, 'Let us pass through your land to get to our land. No one will do you harm; we will simply pass by on foot.' But they refused to open to him. [49] Then Judas ordered proclamation to be made to the army that all should encamp where they were. [50] So the men of the forces encamped, and he fought against the town all that day and all the night, and the town was delivered into his hands. [51] He destroyed every male by the edge of the sword, and razed and plundered the town. Then he passed through the town over the bodies of the dead.

[52] Then they crossed the Jordan into the large plain before Beth-shan. [53] Judas kept rallying the laggards and encouraging the people all the way until he came to the land of Judah. [54] So they went up to Mount Zion with joy and gladness, and offered burnt-offerings, because they had returned in safety; not one of them had fallen.

Joseph and Azariah Defeated

[55] Now while Judas and Jonathan were in Gilead and their brother Simon was in Galilee before Ptolemais, [56] Joseph son of Zechariah, and Azariah, the commanders of the forces, heard of their brave deeds and of the heroic war they had fought. [57] So they said, 'Let us also make a

name for ourselves; let us go and make war on the Gentiles around us.' [58] So they issued orders to the men of the forces that were with them and marched against Jamnia. [59] Gorgias and his men came out of the town to meet them in battle. [60] Then Joseph and Azariah were routed, and were pursued to the borders of Judea; as many as two thousand of the people of Israel fell that day. [61] Thus the people suffered a great rout because, thinking to do a brave deed, they did not listen to Judas and his brothers. [62] But they did not belong to the family of those men through whom deliverance was given to Israel.

[63] The man Judas and his brothers were greatly honoured in all Israel and among all the Gentiles, wherever their name was heard. [64] People gathered to them and praised them.

Success at Hebron and Philistia

[65] Then Judas and his brothers went out and fought the descendants of Esau in the land to the south. He struck Hebron and its villages and tore down its strongholds and burned its towers on all sides. [66] Then he marched off to go into the land of the Philistines, and passed through Marisa. [67] On that day some priests, who wished to do a brave deed, fell in battle, for they went out to battle unwisely. [68] But Judas turned aside to Azotus in the land of the Philistines; he tore down their altars, and the carved images of their gods he burned with fire; he plundered the towns and returned to the land of Judah.

2 Maccabees 10:14-38 New Revised Standard Version, Anglicised Catholic Edition

Campaign in Idumea

[14] When Gorgias became governor of the region, he maintained a force of mercenaries, and at every turn kept attacking the Jews. [15] Besides this, the Idumeans, who had control of important strongholds, were harassing the Jews; they received those who were banished from Jerusalem, and endeavoured to keep up the war. [16] But Maccabeus and his forces, after making solemn supplication and imploring God to fight on their side, rushed to the strongholds of the Idumeans. [17] Attacking them vigorously, they gained possession of the

places, and beat off all who fought upon the wall, and slaughtered those whom they encountered, killing no fewer than twenty thousand.

[18] When at least nine thousand took refuge in two very strong towers well equipped to withstand a siege, [19] Maccabeus left Simon and Joseph, and also Zacchaeus and his troops, a force sufficient to besiege them; and he himself set off for places where he was more urgently needed. [20] But those with Simon, who were money-hungry, were bribed by some of those who were in the towers, and on receiving seventy thousand drachmas let some of them slip away. [21] When word of what had happened came to Maccabeus, he gathered the leaders of the people, and accused these men of having sold their kindred for money by setting their enemies free to fight against them. [22] Then he killed these men who had turned traitor, and immediately captured the two towers. [23] Having success at arms in everything he undertook, he destroyed more than twenty thousand in the two strongholds.

Judas Defeats Timothy

[24] Now Timothy, who had been defeated by the Jews before, gathered a tremendous force of mercenaries and collected the cavalry from Asia in no small number. He came on, intending to take Judea by storm. [25] As he drew near, Maccabeus and his men sprinkled dust on their heads and girded their loins with sackcloth, in supplication to God. [26] Falling upon the steps before the altar, they implored him to be gracious to them and to be an enemy to their enemies and an adversary to their adversaries, as the law declares. [27] And rising from their prayer they took up their arms and advanced a considerable distance from the city; and when they came near the enemy they halted. [28] Just as dawn was breaking, the two armies joined battle, one having as pledge of success and victory not only their valour but also their reliance on the Lord, while the other made rage their leader in the fight.

[29] When the battle became fierce, there appeared to the enemy from heaven five resplendent men on horses with golden bridles, and they were leading the Jews. [30] Two of them took Maccabeus between them, and shielding him with their own armour and weapons, they kept him from being wounded. They showered arrows and thunderbolts on

the enemy, so that, confused and blinded, they were thrown into disorder and cut to pieces. ³¹Twenty thousand five hundred were slaughtered, besides six hundred cavalry.

³²Timothy himself fled to a stronghold called Gazara, especially well garrisoned, where Chaereas was commander. ³³Then Maccabeus and his men were glad, and they besieged the fort for four days. ³⁴The men within, relying on the strength of the place, kept blaspheming terribly and uttering wicked words. ³⁵But at dawn on the fifth day, twenty young men in the army of Maccabeus, fired with anger because of the blasphemies, bravely stormed the wall and with savage fury cut down everyone they met. ³⁶Others who came up in the same way wheeled around against the defenders and set fire to the towers; they kindled fires and burned the blasphemers alive. Others broke open the gates and let in the rest of the force, and they occupied the city. ³⁷They killed Timothy, who was hiding in a cistern, and his brother Chaereas, and Apollophanes. ³⁸When they had accomplished these things, with hymns and thanksgivings they blessed the Lord who shows great kindness to Israel and gives them the victory.

2 Maccabees 12:10-37 New Revised Standard Version, Anglicised Catholic Edition

The Campaign in Gilead

¹⁰When they had gone more than a mile from there, on their march against Timothy, at least five thousand Arabs with five hundred cavalry attacked them. ¹¹After a hard fight, Judas and his companions, with God's help, were victorious. The defeated nomads begged Judas to grant them pledges of friendship, promising to give him livestock and to help his people in all other ways. ¹²Judas, realizing that they might indeed be useful in many ways, agreed to make peace with them; and after receiving his pledges they went back to their tents.

¹³He also attacked a certain town that was strongly fortified with earthworks and walls, and inhabited by all sorts of Gentiles. Its name was Caspin. ¹⁴Those who were within, relying on the strength of the walls and on their supply of provisions, behaved most insolently towards Judas and his men, railing at them and even blaspheming and saying unholy things. ¹⁵But Judas and his men, calling upon the great

Sovereign of the world, who without battering-rams or engines of war overthrew Jericho in the days of Joshua, rushed furiously upon the walls. [16] They took the town by the will of God, and slaughtered untold numbers, so that the adjoining lake, a quarter of a mile wide, appeared to be running over with blood.

Judas Defeats Timothy's Army

[17] When they had gone ninety-five miles from there, they came to Charax, to the Jews who are called Toubiani. [18] They did not find Timothy in that region, for he had by then left there without accomplishing anything, though in one place he had left a very strong garrison. [19] Dositheus and Sosipater, who were captains under Maccabeus, marched out and destroyed those whom Timothy had left in the stronghold, more than ten thousand men. [20] But Maccabeus arranged his army in divisions, set men in command of the divisions, and hurried after Timothy, who had with him one hundred and twenty thousand infantry and two thousand five hundred cavalry. [21] When Timothy learned of the approach of Judas, he sent off the women and the children and also the baggage to a place called Carnaim; for that place was hard to besiege and difficult of access because of the narrowness of all the approaches. [22] But when Judas's first division appeared, terror and fear came over the enemy at the manifestation to them of him who sees all things. In their flight they rushed headlong in every direction, so that often they were injured by their own men and pierced by the points of their own swords. [23] Judas pressed the pursuit with the utmost vigour, putting the sinners to the sword, and destroyed as many as thirty thousand.

[24] Timothy himself fell into the hands of Dositheus and Sosipater and their men. With great guile he begged them to let him go in safety, because he held the parents of most of them, and the brothers of some, to whom no consideration would be shown. [25] And when with many words he had confirmed his solemn promise to restore them unharmed, they let him go, for the sake of saving their kindred.

Judas Wins Other Victories

[26] Then Judas marched against Carnaim and the temple of Atargatis, and slaughtered twenty-five thousand people. [27] After the

rout and destruction of these, he marched also against Ephron, a fortified town where Lysias lived with multitudes of people of all nationalities. Stalwart young men took their stand before the walls and made a vigorous defence; and great stores of war engines and missiles were there. [28] But the Jews called upon the Sovereign who with power shatters the might of his enemies, and they got the town into their hands, and killed as many as twenty-five thousand of those who were in it.

[29] Setting out from there, they hastened to Scythopolis, which is seventy-five miles from Jerusalem. [30] But when the Jews who lived there bore witness to the goodwill that the people of Scythopolis had shown them and their kind treatment of them in times of misfortune, [31] they thanked them and exhorted them to be well disposed to their race in the future also. Then they went up to Jerusalem, as the festival of weeks was close at hand.

Judas Defeats Gorgias

[32] After the festival called Pentecost, they hurried against Gorgias, the governor of Idumea, [33] who came out with three thousand infantry and four hundred cavalry. [34] When they joined battle, it happened that a few of the Jews fell. [35] But a certain Dositheus, one of Bacenor's men, who was on horseback and was a strong man, caught hold of Gorgias, and grasping his cloak was dragging him off by main strength, wishing to take the accursed man alive, when one of the Thracian cavalry bore down on him and cut off his arm; so Gorgias escaped and reached Marisa.

[36] As Esdris and his men had been fighting for a long time and were weary, Judas called upon the Lord to show himself their ally and leader in the battle. [37] In the language of their ancestors he raised the battle-cry, with hymns; then he charged against Gorgias's troops when they were not expecting it and put them to flight.

Background

In 164 BC, the Seleucid Empire, under the leadership of Regent Lysias, launched a major expedition to regain control over the Jewish countryside. This expedition was undertaken while King Antiochus IV was away on campaign in the eastern provinces. However, the Seleucid forces were unsuccessful in their mission due to a combination of factors, including the Battle of Beth Zur and the death of Antiochus IV. Lysias was forced to retreat to the capital city of Antioch to secure his own position as Regent and defend the authority of the young king, Antiochus V Eupator.

The Maccabees, a Jewish rebel group, took advantage of this opportunity to gain control of Jerusalem and expand their influence in the region. With the main Seleucid army occupied elsewhere, the Maccabees were able to conquer territories with minimal resistance from local garrisons and hostile militias.

During this time period, while the majority of the population in Judea were Jews, many outlying regions had substantial Jewish populations but also had a significant number of non-Jews. Relations between Jews and non-Jews had deteriorated significantly due to the radicalization that had occurred as a result of the revolt. As a result, the Maccabees launched campaigns to protect Jewish communities in outlying regions and attack hostile non-Jewish populations.

Military Campaigns

Idumea

The Maccabees, led by Judas Maccabeus (also known as Judah Maccabee), launched a military campaign against the region of Idumea, which was occupied by the Edomites, an ancient people referred to in historical texts as the "descendants of Esau." This reference is an attempt to align the actions of the Maccabees with the heroes of Hebrew scripture. The campaign took place in late 163 BC and, like many of the conflicts of that year, it was more of a raid than an invasion.

1 Maccabees describes the second attack led by Judas as a military action targeting the city of Hebron and its surrounding villages, with the goal of destroying their fortifications and burning their towers. 2 Maccabees also mentions a campaign against the Idumeans and states

that anti-Maccabee Judeans who had fled Jerusalem after its capture by the Maccabees had found refuge among the Idumeans. These exiles were actively working to continue the war against the Hasmoneans, which is why Judas led the campaign against Idumea. The siege of two towers in Idumea took longer than expected and some of the enemy escaped; according to 2 Maccabees, this was due to the misconduct of the commanders who accepted bribes. This account also aligns with the trend in historical texts of assigning blame for setbacks to commanders other than Judas, who is consistently portrayed as both a devout leader and a skilled military strategist.

Ammon and Gilead

The Maccabees, under the leadership of Judas, launched a military campaign in the region of Ammon and Gilead. In Ammon, they clashed with the Baneites, a hostile clan, and Seleucid forces under the command of Timothy of Ammon. Although the main Seleucid army was not present, Timothy would have still had garrisons composed of local soldiers as well as likely some mercenaries under his command. They attacked and successfully captured the city of Jazer but subsequently returned to Judea.

In the Gilead region, local Jews had fortified themselves in a stronghold called Dathema after fighting with local non-Jews and Timothy's forces. They requested assistance from the Maccabees, and Judas and his brother Jonathan Apphus returned to the region with 8,000 soldiers. They met peacefully with the Nabateans, a nearby tribe, and assisted the fortified Jews in the Gilead and the Land of Tob. At the city of Bozrah, the Maccabees "killed every male by the edge of the sword, (..) seized all its spoils, and burned it with fire."

Timothy's army had besieged Dathema with siege weaponry, but Judas successfully relieved the fortress and drove off Timothy's forces. The Maccabees then took control of several towns in the Gilead region, including Maapha, Chaspho, Maked, Bosor, and others, plundering and massacring the populations as they went. Timothy and his forces, reinforced by mercenaries, camped across the river at Raphon. The two sides fought again, and Timothy was once again forced to retreat. The Maccabees subsequently burned the town of Carnaim.

While escorting Jewish refugees back to Judea, the Maccabees encountered resistance at the town of Ephron. After negotiations failed, the Maccabees attacked, plundered, and razed the town, and killed the male inhabitants. The refugees were able to return to Judea safely and successfully, in time to celebrate the Feast of Weeks. The book of 2 Maccabees mentions that the Maccabees passed through the land of the Tobiad Jews in the southern reaches of Ammon, who had a temple at Iraq al-Amir near Jazer that the Maccabees had visited earlier. Although the Tobiads generally favored the Seleucids, it is unclear if any fighting occurred between them and the Maccabee forces.

The depiction of Judas offering terms to the town of Ephron but then burning it down and killing the male inhabitants after negotiations failed, aligns with the portrayal of Judas as the perfect Biblical warrior in the book of 1 Maccabees, in line with the military behavior mandated by Deuteronomy 20:10–20 in the Hebrew Scripture. However, the difference is, God mandated what took place in the canonical Scriptures, and while this history is interesting, it has no mandate by God, it is not God sanctioned. This is not to say that people, families, groups, and even nations don't have the right of self-defense. They do.

Galilee

Simon Thassi, a leader of the Maccabees, led 3,000 soldiers to the region of Galilee to engage in military operations. The campaign was aimed at the local non-Jewish population and Simon's forces pursued them "to the gate of Ptolemais." However, the Maccabees did not lay siege to the city. Additionally, Simon was able to escort a large group of Jewish refugees back to Judea with him, likely as part of the Maccabees' efforts to protect and support Jewish communities in the region.

Coastal Greek Towns

The coast of the Eastern Mediterranean during this era was dominated by Greek-friendly cities that were part of the broader Greek trade network. The Seleucid Empire referred to this region as Paralia. While there were Jewish communities in these cities, they were a minority, and the cities were generally hostile to the Maccabean cause.

Commanders named Joseph and Azariah led an attack on the town of Jamnia (Yavneh) to the west of Judea, but they were repulsed by Seleucid general Gorgias, who also served in other battles of the revolt such as the Battle of Emmaus. The Maccabees suffered 2,000 casualties in their defeat and retreat. Judas later returned to the area personally, but reportedly lost some troops near Marisa. He continued on to the city of Azotus and successfully plundered it before returning to Judea.

The book of 2 Maccabees describes a raid against the cities of Joppa and Jamnia after the residents there murdered some local Jews. According to the book, Judas entered the cities, burned ships in their harbors, and killed the murderers in Joppa but declined to conquer either city. However, the historical accuracy of these successful raids is uncertain, as the book of 1 Maccabees clearly describes Jamnia as not falling to the Maccabees, and Joppa was a fortified port in the era, unlikely to be easily raided.

The book of 1 Maccabees, which is written in an archaic style, refers to this area as the "land of the Philistines" for the same reason as it refers to the Edomites as the "sons of Esau"; the Philistines were an ancient people relegated to history, but the reference evokes the language of ancient Jewish heroes and frames the Maccabean expedition in that context. The author of 1 Maccabees also blames the priests who were killed near Marisa for disobeying orders, but this could be an interpretation, as the author is biased in favor of Judas Maccabeus and may interpret any setbacks as due to defiance of his orders rather than other factors.

Analysis

Scholars have analyzed the historical accounts of the Maccabean campaigns, including the book of 1 Maccabees, which contains brief letters requesting assistance from the Maccabees against Timothy from the Jews of Gilead at Dathema and from the Jews of Galilee. Historian John Grainger, who is skeptical of the reliability of the books of Maccabees, argues that these letters may have been post-factual inventions created to provide additional justification for the expeditions.

Grainger suggests that the expeditions were likely driven by a combination of defensive moves to weaken nearby sources of Seleucid power, an attempt to gather needed manpower for Judas's armies, and a looting expedition. He also argues that these raids probably did not stretch as far as they were claimed to. The book of 1 Maccabees was likely written during the reign of John Hyrcanus, a time when the Hasmonean state had expanded its borders beyond Judea. Grainger suggests that the book may be trying to justify the conquests of the author's time (130–100 BC) by prefiguring them in Judas's time and giving them a moral arc of rescuing fellow Jews and punishing enemies of the Jews.

Fictional Story of the Maccabee Campaigns of 163 BC

It was the year 164 BC, and the Seleucid Empire had sent a powerful expedition to restore order in the Judean countryside. However, the Seleucid force was met with fierce resistance from the Maccabees, a group of Jewish rebels led by Judas Maccabeus, who were determined to defend their homeland and religious freedom.

The Maccabees began their campaign in Idumea, occupied by the Edomites, and known archaically as the "descendants of Esau." Judas and his forces fought bravely, striking Hebron and its villages and tearing down its strongholds and burning its towers on all sides. They were successful in their attack and returned to Judea victorious.

Next, the Maccabees turned their attention to Ammon and Gilead. They clashed with both the Baneites, a hostile clan, and Seleucid forces under Timothy of Ammon. Despite being outnumbered, the Maccabees fought fiercely and were able to capture the city of Jazer. However, they were forced to retreat and return to Judea. But the Maccabees were not done yet, they returned to Gilead to aid the Jews who had fortified themselves in a stronghold called Dathema after fighting with local non-Jews and Timothy's forces.

Judas and his brother Jonathan Apphus returned with 8,000 soldiers and met peaceably with the Nabateans, they aided the fortified Jews in the Gilead and the Land of Tob. At Bozrah, the Maccabees "killed every male by the edge of the sword, (..) seized all its spoils, and burned it with fire." Judas and his forces had just captured the city of Bozrah and killed all the males there. After this, they moved on to other towns in Gilead and continued to plunder and massacre as they went. Timothy and his forces, now made up mostly of mercenaries, camped across the river at Raphon and the two sides fought again. This time, Timothy was again forced back, and the Maccabees burned the town of Carnaim afterwards.

As they escorted Jewish refugees back to Judea, the Maccabees encountered resistance at the town of Ephron. They attacked it, plundered and destroyed the town, and killed the male inhabitants. The refugees returned to Judea safely and successfully, just in time to celebrate the Feast of Weeks.

The Maccabees then led by Simon Thassi, turned their attention to Galilee, where they fought against the local non-Jewish population. They pursued them "to the gate of Ptolemais" but did not besiege the city, and like Judas, Simon was able to escort a large group of Jewish refugees back to Judea with him.

Finally, the Maccabees led by Joseph and Azariah, attacked the coast of the Eastern Mediterranean, which was dominated by Greek-friendly cities who participated in the broader Greek world trading network. They were repelled by the Seleucid general Gorgias and suffered 2,000 casualties in their defeat and retreat. Judas later returned to the area but lost some troops near Marisa and was not able to conquer the towns.

Despite facing many challenges, the Maccabees were able to successfully defend their homeland and protect their fellow Jews, ultimately securing religious freedom for their people.

CHAPTER 11 Battle of Beth Zechariah

Image 20 1698 illustration of Eleazar fighting an elephant at the battle by Jan Luyken

The Battle of Beth Zechariah was a significant engagement that occurred in May 162 BC during the Maccabean Revolt. The Maccabean Revolt was a rebellion led by the Jewish people against the Seleucid Empire, a Greek successor state that controlled Syria and Babylonia. The leader of the Jewish rebels was Judas Maccabeus, also known as Judah Maccabee. The battle took place at Beth Zechariah, which is now known as Khirbet Beit Zakariyyah. Despite the efforts of the Jewish rebels, the Seleucid army emerged victorious. The Jewish rebels were forced to retreat and suffered the loss of Judas's brother, Eleazar Avaran, who was killed in combat while fighting against a war elephant. This defeat allowed the Seleucid army to continue their campaign and lay siege to the Jewish holy city of Jerusalem.

Primary Sources

The Battle of Beth Zechariah, a significant engagement that occurred during the Maccabean Revolt, is recorded in several primary sources. These sources include the book of 1 Maccabees (1 Maccabees 6:28–47), as well as two of Josephus's histories: Antiquities of the Jews Book 12, Chapter 9 and The War of the Jews Book 1.1.41–46. 1 Maccabees is considered to be the main source on the battle and provides a detailed description of the Seleucid forces, indicating that the author may have been an eyewitness or had access to detailed accounts from eyewitnesses. The other primary sources, Antiquities and War of the Jews, largely echo 1 Maccabees, but also include additional details based on Josephus's first-hand knowledge of Judean topography and geography. Additionally, War of the Jews contains new material that is not present in 1 Maccabees, suggesting that Josephus may have used other Greek sources, such as Nicolaus of Damascus, in its composition. 2 Maccabees describes the battle in very general terms (2 Maccabees 13:13–26) and focuses on a raid undertaken by Judas as well as the actions of a Jewish traitor, Rhodocus, who was caught passing secrets to the Seleucids. The author of 2 Maccabees seems to have been aware of the true outcome of the battle but chose to present it in a way that would not be seen as an embarrassing setback for the rebellion. 2 Maccabees also dates the expedition to 149 SE (163 BC), slightly earlier than 1 Maccabees, which is a point of debate among scholars.

1 Maccabees 6:28-47 New Revised Standard Version, Anglicised Catholic Edition

[28] The king was enraged when he heard this. He assembled all his Friends, the commanders of his forces and those in authority. [29] Mercenary forces also came to him from other kingdoms and from islands of the seas. [30] The number of his forces was one

hundred thousand foot-soldiers, twenty thousand horsemen, and thirty-two elephants accustomed to war. [31] They came through Idumea and encamped against Beth-zur, and for many days they fought and built engines of war; but the Jews sallied out and burned these with fire, and fought courageously.

The Battle at Beth-zechariah

[32] Then Judas marched away from the citadel and encamped at Beth-zechariah, opposite the camp of the king. [33] Early in the morning the king set out and took his army by a forced march along the road to Beth-zechariah, and his troops made ready for battle and sounded their trumpets. [34] They offered the elephants the juice of grapes and mulberries, to arouse them for battle. [35] They distributed the animals among the phalanxes; with each elephant they stationed a thousand men armed with coats of mail, and with brass helmets on their heads; and five hundred picked horsemen were assigned to each beast. [36] These took their position beforehand wherever the animal was; wherever it went, they went with it, and they never left it. [37] On the elephants were wooden towers, strong and covered; they were fastened on each animal by special harness, and on each were four armed men who fought from there, and also its Indian driver. [38] The rest of the cavalry were stationed on either side, on the two flanks of the army, to harass the enemy while being themselves protected by the phalanxes. [39] When the sun shone on the shields of gold and brass, the hills were ablaze with them and gleamed like flaming torches.

[40] Now a part of the king's army was spread out on the high hills, and some troops were on the plain, and they advanced steadily and in good order. [41] All who heard the noise made by their multitude, by the marching of the multitude and the clanking of their arms, trembled, for the army was very large and strong. [42] But Judas and his army advanced to the battle, and six hundred of the king's army fell. [43] Now Eleazar, called Avaran, saw that one of the animals was equipped with royal armour. It was taller than all the others, and he supposed that the king was on it. [44] So he gave his life to save his people and to win for himself an everlasting name. [45] He courageously ran into the midst of the phalanx to reach it; he killed men right and left, and they parted

before him on both sides. [46] He got under the elephant, stabbed it from beneath, and killed it; but it fell to the ground upon him and he died. [47] When the Jews saw the royal might and the fierce attack of the forces, they turned away in flight.

2 Maccabees 13:13-26

New Revised Standard Version, Anglicised Catholic Edition

[13] After consulting privately with the elders, he determined to march out and decide the matter by the help of God before the king's army could enter Judea and get possession of the city. [14] So, committing the decision to the Creator of the world and exhorting his troops to fight bravely to the death for the laws, temple, city, country, and commonwealth, he pitched his camp near Modein. [15] He gave his troops the watchword, 'God's victory', and with a picked force of the bravest young men, he attacked the king's pavilion at night and killed as many as two thousand men in the camp. He stabbed the leading elephant and its rider. [16] In the end they filled the camp with terror and confusion and withdrew in triumph. [17] This happened, just as day was dawning, because the Lord's help protected him.

Antiochus Makes a Treaty with the Jews

[18] The king, having had a taste of the daring of the Jews, tried strategy in attacking their positions. [19] He advanced against Beth-zur, a strong fortress of the Jews, was turned back, attacked again, and was defeated. [20] Judas sent in to the garrison whatever was necessary. [21] But Rhodocus, a man from the ranks of the Jews, gave secret information to the enemy; he was sought for, caught, and put in prison. [22] The king negotiated a second time with the people in Beth-zur, gave pledges, received theirs, withdrew, attacked Judas and his men, and was defeated; [23] he got word that Philip, who had been left in charge of the government, had revolted in Antioch; he was dismayed, called in the Jews, yielded and swore to observe all their rights, settled with them and offered sacrifice, honoured the sanctuary, and showed generosity to the holy place. [24] He received Maccabeus, left Hegemonides as governor from Ptolemais to Gerar, [25] and went to Ptolemais. The people of Ptolemais were indignant over the treaty; in fact they were so angry that they wanted to annul its terms. [26] Lysias took the public

platform, made the best possible defence, convinced them, appeased them, gained their goodwill, and set out for Antioch. This is how the king's attack and withdrawal turned out.

Background

The background leading up to the Battle of Beth Zechariah is rooted in the Maccabean Revolt, a rebellion led by the Jewish people against the Seleucid Empire. In autumn 164 BC, the Seleucid Empire's Regent Lysias launched an expedition to Judea to put down the rebellion. The Maccabees, led by Judas Maccabeus, fought against the Greeks at the Battle of Beth Zur. Lysias, either due to losses in the battle or from news of the death of King Antiochus IV, left Judea and negotiated a compromise. He returned to the Seleucid capital of Antioch to fend off a political challenge for leadership from Philip, a prominent official from Media who claimed to have been appointed regent by Antiochus IV before his death. The Maccabees, in the meantime, captured Jerusalem, purified the temple, and rededicated the altar for Jewish worship. However, the Seleucid forces still controlled the Acra, a formidable fortress within the city that faced the Temple Mount. The Maccabees participated in various campaigns across greater Palestine while the Seleucid government was preoccupied with internal politics in the capital. Around April 162 BC, Judas laid siege to the Acra in an attempt to eradicate the most prominent symbol of Seleucid power in Judea. This prompted a strong response from Lysias, who made a second expedition to Judea to relieve the Acra. Both sides struggled with food shortages, with the problem being exacerbated by a wave of Jewish refugees from outlying regions that had been brought to Judea for their own safety as the outlying regions descended into disorder due to raids and civilian violence between the Jewish and Gentile populations. Lysias's expeditionary force was quite large, with estimates of around 50,000 infantry, about 5,000 cavalry, and approximately 80 war elephants. The size of the Jewish army is unknown, but it is speculated that they had trained a Hellenistic-style army in the year and a half since taking Jerusalem, with anywhere from 10,000 to 20,000 soldiers.

Image 21 Eleazar Avaran trampled by a war elephant. Adasa would be the last battle with significant war elephant use for the Seleucids, as the Romans would hamstring the remaining elephants in the next months. Illustration by Gustave Doré in 1866.

Lysias's Expedition

In order to defeat the Maccabean rebellion, Lysias, the Regent of the Seleucid Empire, led an expedition to Judea with a formidable army of Syrian Greeks. They approached Judea from the southwest, through Mount Hebron, and successfully besieged Beth-zur. Afterwards, they continued northward towards Jerusalem, which was about 32 kilometers away. Rather than resorting to the guerrilla tactics used earlier in the revolt, Judas Maccabeus rallied an army to intercept the expedition and positioned his troops on high ground along the main road to Jerusalem in an effort to restrict the Seleucid's numerical advantage and force them to enter via a narrow valley approach.

In May 162 BC, the two armies clashed at a pass near Beth Zechariah. Lysias sent a force to take the nearby ridges to cover his main force's advance and their flanks, likely his cavalry and possibly skirmishers. The high ground provided better visibility and scouting for the battle's progress. Lysias's army comprised of light infantry at the front, war elephants, and a Greek phalanx armed with sarissas behind. The Jewish army was unnerved by the war elephants, causing them to break and retreat. Judas's brother, Eleazar Avaran, attempted to show his fellow soldiers that the elephants were vulnerable by charging into the mouth of the Syrian forces and attacking a large elephant, but he was killed by the animal.

The Jewish forces collapsed under the heavy pressure of the Greek phalanx, and the Maccabees retreated to mountainous and defensible Aphairema, near the original center of the revolt. Lysias then marched north to Jerusalem and laid siege to the rebel forces there. However, Lysias was limited by time as he couldn't spend too long away from the capital without risking his position as leader. Both sides were running short on food. The siege eventually ended with a peace deal where Lysias agreed to end his siege of Jerusalem, and the Maccabees ended their siege of the Acra. Lysias confirmed the repeal of Antiochus IV's anti-Jewish decrees and the Greeks tore down a defensive wall at "Mount Zion," possibly referring to the Temple Mount. With the peace deal in place, Lysias was able to return to Antioch to fend off a renewed challenge from Philip for leadership of the Seleucid empire and guardianship of the young Antiochus V Eupator. He left around June or July 162 BC, although he may have sent some of his forces back earlier. According to Josephus, Philip was captured and executed, but it is unclear whether Josephus had some unknown and lost source for Philip's eventual fate or this was simply a conjecture based on the fact that Philip never did attain leadership of the Empire.

Analysis

In the analysis of the Battle of Beth Zechariah, it is important to note that 2 Maccabees 13:2 writes that 300 scythed chariots were deployed as part of the expedition. However, this information is doubted by scholars as scythed chariots were generally used for lowland combat on flat plains, and the ground in Judea is not very level, making it difficult to accelerate the chariots to the speed needed to make them effective. Additionally, it is uncertain that the Seleucids even had so many chariots to send, even if they wanted to. Neither 1 Maccabees nor Josephus mention chariots, with both sources being more interested in military details. While Polybius describes 140 chariots at the military parade at Daphne in 166-165 BC, he does not indicate scythes on them, and it is possible that these were merely ceremonial and utilitarian chariots meant for normal transportation rather than warfare.

1 Maccabees describes a larger army than Josephus does, saying that the expedition consisted of one hundred thousand foot-soldiers, twenty thousand horsemen, and thirty-two elephants. Scholars believe these numbers are likely exaggerated, as such manpower likely exceeds the entire Seleucid army, and if actually sent, would have been even more of a logistics nightmare to feed and supply than Josephus's suggestion of 50,000 infantry and 5,000 cavalry. The number of elephants is also uncertain; Josephus writes that eighty elephants were with the expedition, although historian Bezalel Bar-Kochva argues for a lower figure. He suggests that Josephus might have misread an "8" as an "80" and notes that only 36-42 elephants were recorded by Polybius at the Daphne parade.

A point of uncertainty in the conflict between Eleazar and the elephant is that 1 Maccabees writes that "the king" was on the elephant that Eleazar attacked. The ten-year old king is not described as accompanying the expedition. It is possible that the term "king" referred to the regent, and Eleazar somehow thought that Lysias or some other important commander must have been on the elephant, perhaps due to some impressive royal seal or decoration, but it is unclear if Eleazar's belief was correct or not, as Hellenistic commanders almost always rode on horses in the style of Alexander the Great. Additionally, 1 Maccabees also describes the elephant as dying "instantly," which is likely an exaggeration from the fog of war. The elephant may have eventually died, but as elephant hunters can attest, they do not die quickly or easily. With the technology of the era, only an arrow fired nearly point-blank from a powerful bow to the brain or heart could instantly fell an elephant, and even a grave abdominal wound could take a few hours to bleed the elephant to death.

Another point of uncertainty is when Alcimus would come to power as High Priest. According to 1 Maccabees, it is only after Demetrius I Soter comes to power, suggesting a later date of 162-161 BC. However, 2 Maccabees suggests Alcimus was appointed during Antiochus V's reign. If the version in 2 Maccabees is trusted, then it is possible that Lysias arranged for Alcimus to be High Priest as part of the peace deal that concluded his expedition. These are all important points of consideration when analyzing the Battle of Beth Zechariah and the context surrounding it.

Legacy

The Battle of Beth Zechariah had a significant impact on the legacy of war elephants in ancient warfare. Following the battle, the Seleucid Empire may have been banned from using war elephants by the Treaty of Apamea, a peace treaty that ended the Roman-Seleucid War in 188 BC. The treaty required the Seleucids to give up their war elephants, and the Romans sent a delegation in 162 BC to enforce the treaty and hamstrung or burned any remaining elephants they could find. As a result, the Battle of Beth Zechariah was one of the last battles where the Seleucids were able to deploy a significant force of war elephants, and their use in warfare became rarer.

In terms of cultural legacy, the Maccabees, including Judas Maccabeus and Eleazar Avaran, have been more frequently depicted in Christian art and literature than in Jewish works. This is due to the fact that the Hasmoneans, the dynasty founded by the Maccabees, were not well-regarded by Jewish rabbis and sages who compiled the Jewish canon after the fall of the Hasmonean kingdom. However, in more recent times, Jews have returned to the topic of the Maccabean Revolt in literature and art. Eleazar's heroism in the Battle of Beth Zechariah was even commemorated in a Hanukkah coin issued by the Bank of Israel in 1961. The town of Elazar in the West Bank was named after him, and the small Arab hamlet of Hirbeit Zakariya is believed to be the location of ancient Beth Zechariah.

Fictional Story of the Battle of Beth Zechariah

The sun was setting over the small village of Beth Zechariah as Judas Maccabeus and his band of Jewish rebels prepared for battle. They had been waiting for weeks for the Seleucid army to arrive, and now, as the dust on the horizon grew closer, they knew that the time had come.

Judas rallied his troops, reminding them of the importance of their mission. They were fighting not just for their own freedom, but for the freedom of all Jews. He reminded them of the atrocities that the Seleucids had committed against their people - the desecration of the temple, the forced worship of Greek gods, and the murder of innocent men, women, and children.

As the Seleucid army approached, Judas ordered his men to take up their positions on the high ground overlooking the main road to Jerusalem. He knew that the Seleucids would be at a disadvantage, forced to march through the narrow valley with their heavy infantry and war elephants. He also knew that his men were outnumbered and outmatched, but he was determined to fight until the bitter end.

The Seleucid army arrived in the early morning, and the battle began. The Jewish rebels fought bravely, but they were no match for the heavily armed and well-trained Seleucid soldiers. The Seleucid's war elephants caused chaos among the Jewish lines, and many of Judas's men began to flee in fear.

As the battle raged on, Judas's brother, Eleazar Avaran, decided to take matters into his own hands. He saw that the elephants were the key to the Seleucid's success and knew that if he could take out even one of them, it could turn the tide of the battle. So, he rallied a group of men and charged into the mouth of the Seleucid forces.

With a fierce determination in his eyes, Eleazar made his way towards one of the largest elephants. The elephant trumpeted in anger as it prepared to trample Eleazar, but he was undeterred. With a mighty leap, he cast himself under the animal and thrust his sword into its belly. The elephant let out a deafening cry as it fell to the ground, crushing Eleazar underneath.

The death of the elephant had a profound effect on the Jewish rebels. They saw that even the mighty Seleucid war elephants were not invincible and were spurred on by Eleazar's sacrifice. They fought with renewed vigor, and the Seleucids were forced to retreat.

The battle of Beth Zechariah was a turning point in the Maccabean revolt. The Jewish rebels had shown that they could stand up to the powerful Seleucid army and had dealt a significant blow to their morale. Judas and his men were hailed as heroes, and the memory of Eleazar's sacrifice lived on as an inspiration to future generations.

The Seleucids continued to campaign in Judea but the Maccabees were able to take back Jerusalem, they cleansed the temple and rededicated the altar for Jewish worship. The Seleucids eventually retreated, and the Jewish people were able to reclaim their religious and cultural heritage. The Battle of Beth Zechariah became a symbol of hope and resilience for the Jewish people, and it was remembered for centuries to come.

CHAPTER 12 Battle of Adasa

Image 22 Judas is presented with a divine golden sword while asleep. Woodcut by Julius Schnorr von Carolsfeld from the 1860 Die Bibel in Bildern [de]

The Battle of Adasa occurred on the 13th of the month of Adar in 161 BC and took place at the location of Adasa, near Beth-horon. This battle was part of the Maccabean revolt, a rebellion led by Judas Maccabeus (also known as Judah Maccabee) against the Seleucid Empire. The Seleucid army was commanded by a man named Nicanor. The Maccabees emerged victorious in the battle, with Nicanor being killed early in the fighting. This battle was the result of months of political maneuvering, as the peace deal established a year prior by Lysias was challenged by new leaders such as Alcimus, Nicanor, and Judas Maccabeus. The date of the battle in the Hebrew calendar, 13

Adar, is celebrated as Yom Nicanor, or the "Day of Nicanor," to commemorate the Maccabees' victory.

Primary Sources

Primary sources for information on Nicanor's military governance of Judea, the Battle of Caphar-salama, and the Battle of Adasa can be found in several historical texts. These include the books of 1 Maccabees (1 Maccabees 7:26–50) and 2 Maccabees (2 Maccabees 14:12–33, 2 Maccabees 15:1–36), as well as in Josephus's Antiquities of the Jews Book 12, Chapter 10. These texts provide varying levels of detail about the battles. The Battle of Caphar-salama is described with relatively little information, which could be due to the fact that it was a short and one-sided battle, the author of 1 Maccabees was not present for it, or both. The Battle of Adasa is described with slightly more detail, but mainly in regards to the geographic region where it took place. The authors of these texts instead chose to focus more on the political maneuvering between Nicanor, Alcimus, and Judas.

1 Maccabees 7:26-50 New Revised Standard Version, Anglicised Catholic Edition

Nicanor in Judea

[26] Then the king sent Nicanor, one of his honoured princes, who hated and detested Israel, and he commanded him to destroy the people. [27] So Nicanor came to Jerusalem with a large force, and treacherously sent to Judas and his brothers this peaceable message, [28] 'Let there be no fighting between you and me; I shall come with a few men to see you face to face in peace.'

[29] So he came to Judas, and they greeted one another peaceably; but the enemy were preparing to kidnap Judas. [30] It became known to Judas that Nicanor had come to him with treacherous intent, and he was afraid of him and would not meet him again. [31] When Nicanor learned that his plan had been disclosed, he went out to meet Judas in battle near Caphar-salama. [32] About five hundred of the army of Nicanor fell, and the rest fled into the city of David.

Nicanor Threatens the Temple

[33] After these events Nicanor went up to Mount Zion. Some of the priests from the sanctuary and some of the elders of the people came out to greet him peaceably and to show him the burnt-offering that was being offered for the king. [34] But he mocked them and derided them and defiled them and spoke arrogantly, [35] and in anger he swore this oath, 'Unless Judas and his army are delivered into my hands this time, then if I return safely I will burn up this house.' And he went out in great anger. [36] At this the priests went in and stood before the altar and the temple; they wept and said,

[37] 'You chose this house to be called by your name,
   and to be for your people a house of prayer and supplication.
[38] Take vengeance on this man and on his army,
   and let them fall by the sword;
remember their blasphemies,
   and let them live no longer.'

The Death of Nicanor

[39] Now Nicanor went out from Jerusalem and encamped in Beth-horon, and the Syrian army joined him. [40] Judas encamped in Adasa with three thousand men. Then Judas prayed and said, [41] 'When the messengers from the king spoke blasphemy, your angel went out and struck down one hundred and eighty-five thousand of the Assyrians. [42] So also crush this army before us today; let the rest learn that Nicanor has spoken wickedly against the sanctuary, and judge him according to this wickedness.'

[43] So the armies met in battle on the thirteenth day of the month of Adar. The army of Nicanor was crushed, and he himself was the first to fall in the battle. [44] When his army saw that Nicanor had fallen, they threw down their arms and fled. [45] The Jews pursued them a day's journey, from Adasa as far as Gazara, and as they followed they kept sounding the battle-call on the trumpets. [46] People came out of all the surrounding villages of Judea, and they outflanked the enemy and drove them back to their pursuers, so that they all fell by the sword; not even one of them was left. [47] Then the Jews seized the spoils and the plunder; they cut off Nicanor's head and the right hand that he had

so arrogantly stretched out, and brought them and displayed them just outside Jerusalem. [48] The people rejoiced greatly and celebrated that day as a day of great gladness. [49] They decreed that this day should be celebrated each year on the thirteenth day of Adar. [50] So the land of Judah had rest for a few days.

2 Maccabees 14:12-33 New Revised Standard Version, Anglicised Catholic Edition

[12] He immediately chose Nicanor, who had been in command of the elephants, appointed him governor of Judea, and sent him off [13] with orders to kill Judas and scatter his troops, and to instal Alcimus as high priest of the great temple. [14] And the Gentiles throughout Judea, who had fled before Judas, flocked to join Nicanor, thinking that the misfortunes and calamities of the Jews would mean prosperity for themselves.

Nicanor Makes Friends with Judas

[15] When the Jews heard of Nicanor's coming and the gathering of the Gentiles, they sprinkled dust on their heads and prayed to him who established his own people for ever and always upholds his own heritage by manifesting himself. [16] At the command of the leader, they set out from there immediately and engaged them in battle at a village called Dessau. [17] Simon, the brother of Judas, had encountered Nicanor, but had been temporarily checked because of the sudden consternation created by the enemy.

[18] Nevertheless Nicanor, hearing of the valour of Judas and his troops and their courage in battle for their country, shrank from deciding the issue by bloodshed. [19] Therefore he sent Posidonius, Theodotus, and Mattathias to give and receive pledges of friendship. [20] When the terms had been fully considered, and the leader had informed the people, and it had appeared that they were of one mind, they agreed to the covenant. [21] The leaders set a day on which to meet by themselves. A chariot came forward from each army; seats of honour were set in place; [22] Judas posted armed men in readiness at key places to prevent sudden treachery on the part of the enemy; so they duly held the consultation.

²³ Nicanor stayed on in Jerusalem and did nothing out of the way, but dismissed the flocks of people that had gathered. ²⁴ And he kept Judas always in his presence; he was warmly attached to the man. ²⁵ He urged him to marry and have children; so Judas married, settled down, and shared the common life.

Nicanor Turns against Judas

²⁶ But when Alcimus noticed their goodwill for one another, he took the covenant that had been made and went to Demetrius. He told him that Nicanor was disloyal to the government, since he had appointed that conspirator against the kingdom, Judas, to be his successor. ²⁷ The king became excited and, provoked by the false accusations of that depraved man, wrote to Nicanor, stating that he was displeased with the covenant and commanding him to send Maccabeus to Antioch as a prisoner without delay.

²⁸ When this message came to Nicanor, he was troubled and grieved that he had to annul their agreement when the man had done no wrong. ²⁹ Since it was not possible to oppose the king, he watched for an opportunity to accomplish this by a stratagem. ³⁰ But Maccabeus, noticing that Nicanor was more austere in his dealings with him and was meeting him more rudely than had been his custom, concluded that this austerity did not spring from the best motives. So he gathered not a few of his men, and went into hiding from Nicanor. ³¹ When the latter became aware that he had been cleverly outwitted by the man, he went to the great and holy temple while the priests were offering the customary sacrifices, and commanded them to hand the man over. ³² When they declared on oath that they did not know where the man was whom he wanted, ³³ he stretched out his right hand towards the sanctuary, and swore this oath: 'If you do not hand Judas over to me as a prisoner, I will level this shrine of God to the ground and tear down the altar, and build here a splendid temple to Dionysus.'

Image 23 Hartmann-schedel_DESTRVCCIO-IHEROSOLIME 1493

2 Maccabees 15:1-36 New Revised Standard Version, Anglicised Catholic Edition

Nicanor's Arrogance

15 When Nicanor heard that Judas and his troops were in the region of Samaria, he made plans to attack them with complete safety on the day of rest. ²When the Jews who were compelled to follow him said, 'Do not destroy so savagely and barbarously, but show respect for the day that he who sees all things has honoured and hallowed above other days', ³the thrice-accursed wretch asked if there were a sovereign in heaven who had commanded the keeping of the sabbath day. ⁴When they declared, 'It is the living Lord himself, the Sovereign in heaven, who ordered us to observe the seventh day,' ⁵he replied, 'But I am a sovereign also, on earth, and I command you to take up arms and finish the king's business.' Nevertheless, he did not succeed in carrying out his abominable design.

Judas Prepares the Jews for Battle

⁶This Nicanor in his utter boastfulness and arrogance had determined to erect a public monument of victory over Judas and his forces. ⁷But Maccabeus did not cease to trust with all confidence that he would get help from the Lord. ⁸He exhorted his troops not to fear the attack of the Gentiles, but to keep in mind the former times when

help had come to them from heaven, and so to look for the victory that the Almighty would give them. [9] Encouraging them from the law and the prophets, and reminding them also of the struggles they had won, he made them the more eager. [10] When he had aroused their courage, he issued his orders, at the same time pointing out the perfidy of the Gentiles and their violation of oaths. [11] He armed each of them not so much with confidence in shields and spears as with the inspiration of brave words, and he cheered them all by relating a dream, a sort of vision, which was worthy of belief.

[12] What he saw was this: Onias, who had been high priest, a noble and good man, of modest bearing and gentle manner, one who spoke fittingly and had been trained from childhood in all that belongs to excellence, was praying with outstretched hands for the whole body of the Jews. [13] Then in the same fashion another appeared, distinguished by his grey hair and dignity, and of marvellous majesty and authority. [14] And Onias spoke, saying, 'This is a man who loves the family of Israel and prays much for the people and the holy city—Jeremiah, the prophet of God.' [15] Jeremiah stretched out his right hand and gave to Judas a golden sword, and as he gave it he addressed him thus: [16] 'Take this holy sword, a gift from God, with which you will strike down your adversaries.'

[17] Encouraged by the words of Judas, so noble and so effective in arousing valour and awaking courage in the souls of the young, they determined not to carry on a campaign but to attack bravely, and to decide the matter by fighting hand to hand with all courage, because the city and the sanctuary and the temple were in danger. [18] Their concern for wives and children, and also for brothers and sisters and relatives, lay upon them less heavily; their greatest and first fear was for the consecrated sanctuary. [19] And those who had to remain in the city were in no little distress, being anxious over the encounter in the open country.

The Defeat and Death of Nicanor

[20] When all were now looking forward to the coming issue, and the enemy was already close at hand with their army drawn up for battle, the elephants strategically stationed and the cavalry deployed on

the flanks, [21] Maccabeus, observing the masses that were in front of him and the varied supply of arms and the savagery of the elephants, stretched out his hands towards heaven and called upon the Lord who works wonders; for he knew that it is not by arms, but as the Lord decides, that he gains the victory for those who deserve it. [22] He called upon him in these words: 'O Lord, you sent your angel in the time of King Hezekiah of Judea, and he killed fully one hundred and eighty-five thousand in the camp of Sennacherib. [23] So now, O Sovereign of the heavens, send a good angel to spread terror and trembling before us. [24] By the might of your arm may these blasphemers who come against your holy people be struck down.' With these words he ended his prayer.

[25] Nicanor and his troops advanced with trumpets and battle-songs, [26] but Judas and his troops met the enemy in battle with invocations to God and prayers. [27] So, fighting with their hands and praying to God in their hearts, they laid low at least thirty-five thousand, and were greatly gladdened by God's manifestation.

[28] When the action was over and they were returning with joy, they recognized Nicanor, lying dead, in full armour. [29] Then there was shouting and tumult, and they blessed the Sovereign Lord in the language of their ancestors. [30] Then the man who was ever in body and soul the defender of his people, the man who maintained his youthful goodwill towards his compatriots, ordered them to cut off Nicanor's head and arm and carry them to Jerusalem. [31] When he arrived there and had called his compatriots together and stationed the priests before the altar, he sent for those who were in the citadel. [32] He showed them the vile Nicanor's head and that profane man's arm, which had been boastfully stretched out against the holy house of the Almighty. [33] He cut out the tongue of the ungodly Nicanor and said that he would feed it piecemeal to the birds and would hang up these rewards of his folly opposite the sanctuary. [34] And they all, looking to heaven, blessed the Lord who had manifested himself, saying, 'Blessed is he who has kept his own place undefiled!' [35] Judas hung Nicanor's head from the citadel, a clear and conspicuous sign to everyone of the help of the Lord. [36] And they all decreed by public vote never to let this day go unobserved, but to celebrate the thirteenth day of the twelfth

month—which is called Adar in the Aramaic language—the day before Mordecai's day.

Nicanor's Governorship

In 162 BC, Regent Lysias led an expedition to regain control of Judea and lift the siege of the Acra citadel in Jerusalem. After the Maccabees were defeated in the Battle of Beth Zechariah, they were forced to retreat. However, Lysias's return to the Seleucid capital of Antioch was expedited due to political considerations. Despite fending off a challenge from a Seleucid leader named Philip, a greater threat emerged soon after in the form of Demetrius I Soter. Demetrius, the son of Seleucus IV, had escaped captivity in Rome with the help of the Greek historian Polybius and returned to Syria. He successfully convinced the Greek leaders of Antioch to support him, and he took the throne, ordering the arrest and execution of Antiochus V and Lysias. This action strained relations between the Seleucid Empire and the Roman Republic, and Rome began to offer support to potential sources of rebellion and disunity within the Seleucid Empire, such as Timarchus, Ptolemaus of Commagene, and the Maccabees.

Demetrius's first move in regards to the situation in Judea was to send a new military expedition there under Seleucid general Bacchides. The size and scope of the expedition is unknown, but one of its purposes was to install Alcimus as High Priest of Judea. Alcimus was a moderate Hellenizer who worked to divide Jewish support for the Maccabees, and he was apparently successful to some extent. Tensions continued to simmer between the Maccabees in the countryside, the moderate Hellenist Jews in the cities, and the Greeks.

Against this backdrop, Nicanor was appointed strategos (general/governor) of the region, likely ruling from the Acra. Nicanor had previously been a commander of Seleucid war elephants and had taken part in the Battle of Emmaus four years earlier. On his way to assume the governorship, he fought a skirmish with Maccabee forces under Simon Thassi (Simeon) at a place called Dessau or Caphardessau, and Nicanor won, forcing the Maccabees to retreat.

As part of his governorship, Nicanor attempted to negotiate and even befriend Judas, according to 2 Maccabees. Judas was even given an official government role, and he was tentatively involved in the administration and management of Judea. However, a rivalry between Nicanor and Alcimus undid this potential warming of relations. Alcimus, perhaps worried about being replaced or his authority being undermined, complained to the authorities in Antioch. New orders from Demetrius at the behest of this rivalry forced Nicanor to move more aggressively against Judas. Realizing something had changed, Judas retreated back to the countryside where his remaining army waited.

Caphar-Salama and Adasa

Nicanor, with a small force, set out from Jerusalem to track down Judas and the rebels. At Caphar-salama, a skirmish was fought, in which the Seleucids suffered 500 casualties and were forced to retreat back to Jerusalem. Nicanor is said to have then made a threat to the priests at the Second Temple, threatening to burn it down if they did not help him find Judas. The veracity of this account is unclear, as the surviving sources have a hostile view of Nicanor, and the priests at the Temple would have likely been subordinates of Alcimus.

Regardless, Nicanor's actions earned him the hatred of the rebels. He then camped in the region of Beth-horon, northwest of Jerusalem, to meet with Seleucid reinforcements traveling from Samaria. The rebels set their forces against him at Adasa. According to 2 Maccabees 15, Judas inspired his troops by relating to them a dream-vision he had experienced, in which the Prophet Jeremiah presented him with a gold sword and said, "Take this holy sword, a gift from God, with which you will strike down your adversaries." The battle appears to have been a direct frontal confrontation, and Nicanor was killed early in the battle, which caused the Seleucid force to retreat. The Seleucid troops retreated toward Gazara, the nearest Seleucid fortress to the west around 30 kilometers away. The Jewish army followed in pursuit and Jewish partisans in the nearby towns harried their retreat, inflicting significant casualties on the fleeing government army.

Aftermath

After the Battle of Adasa, Nicanor's body was desecrated as a form of punishment and to raise the morale of the rebels. His head and right hand were cut off, a Persian punishment, and displayed near Jerusalem, as he was the first high-ranking officer killed by the Maccabees. The victory at Adasa also allowed Judas Maccabeus to negotiate with the Romans from a position of greater strength, and he was able to extract a weak promise of potential Roman support in the future against Demetrius. However, King Demetrius would suppress the rebellion of Timarchus in the eastern satrapies around early 160 BC, freeing up soldiers for other tasks such as suppressing the Judean unrest. Despite the victory at Adasa, Judas Maccabeus was defeated and killed in the Battle of Elasa a year later.

Analysis

The location of the battle at Dessau, where Simon fought Nicanor before he assumed the governorship, is unknown. Some scholars speculate that the location may have been confused with Caphar-salama, but there is no clear evidence to support this. The historical accuracy of the negotiations between Nicanor and Judas is also debated among scholars, with some believing that the depiction in 1 Maccabees is more reliable, while others argue that 2 Maccabees provides a more accurate account.

The Battle of Adasa itself was a small-scale engagement, with estimates for the size of the Judean army ranging from 2,000 to 3,000 soldiers, and the Seleucid army estimated at around 9,000 soldiers. However, some historians believe these estimates to be too low and that Judas would not have engaged in an open battle if he was heavily outnumbered. The presence of war elephants on the Seleucid side is also considered doubtful, as there is no clear evidence to support this claim.

The story of the Prophet Jeremiah bestowing a divine sword to Judas as a sign of God's favor is also seen as a literary device to bolster Judas's authority as a leader. The date of the battle is given as 13 Adar, but the year is not specified, leading to some uncertainty about the duration of Nicanor's governorship.

Legacy

The victory at the Battle of Adasa led to the creation of a Jewish festival called Yom Nicanor, or the Day of Nicanor, to commemorate the defeat of Nicanor, who had threatened to burn the Temple, and the return of Judas Maccabeus to Jerusalem after a period of Seleucid rule. The festival is held on the 13th of Adar, the day of the battle. It still has a place in the Jewish calendar of special days, known as "Megillat Ta'anit." Later rabbinical writings, such as in the Ta'anit tractate of the Talmud, focus more on Nicanor's arrogance and threats backfiring on him, rather than the actions of Judas Maccabeus. This may have been an attempt to counterbalance the Hasmonean aggrandizement of the book of 1 Maccabees and avoid hero-worship of Judas. The Battle of Adasa and the Jewish resistance against the Seleucids is considered to be a significant event in Jewish history, as it marked a major victory for the Maccabees and helped to secure Jewish independence.

Fictional Story of the Battle of Adasa

Once upon a time, in the land of Judea, the Seleucid Empire ruled with an iron fist. The people, especially the Jews, were tired of being oppressed and longed for freedom. One day, a brave leader named Judas Maccabeus emerged, determined to fight for the freedom of his people.

Judas rallied his army and began to fight against the Seleucids, winning several battles and gaining the support of the people. But their greatest challenge was yet to come - the Battle of Adasa.

The Seleucid army was led by a ruthless general named Nicanor, who was determined to crush the rebellion once and for all. On the 13th of Adar, the two armies met in the fields of Adasa, ready for a fierce battle.

As the fighting began, Nicanor could be seen on the front lines, his war elephants trampling anything in their path. But Judas had a secret weapon - a vision from the Prophet Jeremiah, who had given him a golden sword, a gift from God.

With the sword in hand, Judas charged towards Nicanor, and a fierce battle ensued. But Judas was able to strike down Nicanor early in the fight, and the Seleucid army was thrown into chaos.

The Maccabees fought with all their might, and soon the Seleucids were in full retreat. The people of Judea had won a great victory, and Judas was hailed as a hero.

After the battle, Nicanor's head and right hand were cut off and displayed as a warning to other Seleucid generals who dare to threaten the Temple. The people celebrated their victory and honored the memory of those who had fallen in the Battle of Adasa.

From that day on, the 13th of Adar was celebrated as Yom Nicanor, a day to commemorate the victory and the freedom of the Jewish people. Judas continued to lead his people and fought for their freedom, but despite the victory at Adasa, he and his army would face many more challenges in the coming years. But the memory of the Battle of Adasa and the bravery of Judas and his army would never be forgotten, and the Jewish people would always remember the day they won their freedom.

CHAPTER 13 Battle of Elasa

Image 24 A rough reconstruction of the line of Bacchides' march (red line) in his second expedition

The Battle of Elasa was a significant engagement in the Maccabean Revolt, a Jewish rebellion against the Seleucid Empire. The battle was fought in April 160 BC, and was led on the Jewish side by Judas Maccabeus (also known as Judah Maccabee), and on the Seleucid side by Bacchides. The Maccabees were a group of Jewish rebels who sought to reclaim their independence and religious freedom from the Seleucid Empire. The Battle of Elasa was one of a series of engagements fought by Judas Maccabeus, who emerged as a powerful leader and military commander during the revolt. The Maccabees were ultimately successful in their rebellion and established an independent Jewish state known as the Hasmonean Kingdom.

Primary Sources

The primary source for the Battle of Elasa is the First Book of Maccabees which is considered a historical book written in Hebrew by an anonymous author, it is part of the apocryphal or deuterocanonical books of the Bible. It provides an account of the Maccabean Revolt, including the Battle of Elasa. The book is considered to be written around 100 BC, so it is not a contemporary source to the events described but is a relatively early account of the revolt. The book is considered to be relatively accurate and detailed in its description of the events, but since it is written from a Jewish perspective and its author is not known, some bias may be present.

Another primary source is the works of the Jewish historian Josephus, who wrote about the Maccabean Revolt in his book "The Jewish War" and "Antiquities of the Jews" which were written in the 1st century CE, several decades after the events. Josephus' works provide a detailed account of the Maccabean Revolt and the Battle of Elasa. He was a Jewish general, and a historian and his works were written in Greek, but he had access to Jewish sources, yet his works are considered biased towards the Roman Empire.

Both the First Book of Maccabees and Josephus' works are considered reliable sources of information on the Maccabean Revolt and the Battle of Elasa, although they should be read with an awareness of their respective perspectives and potential biases.

1 Maccabees 9:1-22 New Revised Standard Version, Anglicised Catholic Edition

Bacchides Returns to Judea

9 When Demetrius heard that Nicanor and his army had fallen in battle, he sent Bacchides and Alcimus into the land of Judah a second time, and with them the right wing of the army. [2] They went by the road that leads to Gilgal and encamped against Mesaloth in Arbela, and they took it and killed many people. [3] In the first month of the one hundred and fifty-second year they encamped against Jerusalem; [4] then they marched off and went to Berea with twenty thousand foot-soldiers and two thousand cavalry.

⁵ Now Judas was encamped in Elasa, and with him were three thousand picked men. ⁶ When they saw the huge number of the enemy forces, they were greatly frightened, and many slipped away from the camp, until no more than eight hundred of them were left.

⁷ When Judas saw that his army had slipped away and the battle was imminent, he was crushed in spirit, for he had no time to assemble them. ⁸ He became faint, but he said to those who were left, 'Let us get up and go against our enemies. We may have the strength to fight them.' ⁹ But they tried to dissuade him, saying, 'We do not have the strength. Let us rather save our own lives now, and let us come back with our kindred and fight them; we are too few.' ¹⁰ But Judas said, 'Far be it from us to do such a thing as to flee from them. If our time has come, let us die bravely for our kindred, and leave no cause to question our honour.'

The Last Battle of Judas

¹¹ Then the army of Bacchides marched out from the camp and took its stand for the encounter. The cavalry was divided into two companies, and the slingers and the archers went ahead of the army, as did all the chief warriors. ¹² Bacchides was on the right wing. Flanked by the two companies, the phalanx advanced to the sound of the trumpets; and the men with Judas also blew their trumpets. ¹³ The earth was shaken by the noise of the armies, and the battle raged from morning until evening.

¹⁴ Judas saw that Bacchides and the strength of his army were on the right; then all the stout-hearted men went with him, ¹⁵ and they crushed the right wing, and he pursued them as far as Mount Azotus. ¹⁶ When those on the left wing saw that the right wing was crushed, they turned and followed close behind Judas and his men. ¹⁷ The battle became desperate, and many on both sides were wounded and fell. ¹⁸ Judas also fell, and the rest fled.

¹⁹ Then Jonathan and Simon took their brother Judas and buried him in the tomb of their ancestors at Modein, ²⁰ and wept for him. All Israel made great lamentation for him; they mourned for many days and said,

[21] 'How is the mighty fallen,
  the saviour of Israel!'

[22] Now the rest of the acts of Judas, and his wars and the brave deeds that he did, and his greatness, have not been recorded, but they were very many.

Background

The Battle of Elasa took place during the Maccabean Revolt, which was a Jewish rebellion against the Seleucid Empire. The Seleucid Empire was a Hellenistic state that emerged after the death of Alexander the Great in 323 BC. It controlled much of the territory of the former Achaemenid Persian Empire, including Palestine, where the Jewish people lived. The Seleucids attempted to impose their Greek culture and religion on the Jewish population, which led to resistance and rebellion.

The Maccabean Revolt was led by a family of Jewish priests known as the Maccabees, who sought to reclaim Jewish independence and religious freedom from the Seleucids. The rebellion began in 167 BC, when the Seleucid king Antiochus IV Epiphanes attempted to forcefully Hellenize the Jewish population, including outlawing Jewish religious practices and desecrating the Temple in Jerusalem. The rebellion was led by Judas Maccabeus, who emerged as a powerful leader and military commander. The Battle of Elasa was one of a series of engagements fought by Judas Maccabeus and his followers, which ultimately led to the defeat of the Seleucids and the establishment of an independent Jewish state known as the Hasmonean Kingdom.

The cultural context of the battle was the struggle of Jewish people to maintain their religious and cultural identity under the rule of the Seleucids who wanted to hellenize the population and religious practices. The Maccabean Revolt was not only a political struggle, but also a religious and cultural one. The Maccabees were fighting not only for political independence but also for the preservation of their religious traditions and identity.

In addition, the Maccabean Revolt had a significant impact on the development of Jewish culture and religion. The successful rebellion led to the rededication of the Temple in Jerusalem, an event commemorated in the Jewish festival of Hanukkah. The Hasmonean Kingdom also became a major center of Jewish scholarship and learning, and the Maccabees are remembered as heroes in Jewish tradition. The Battle of Elasa was one of the key events in the Maccabean Revolt and had a significant impact on the development of Jewish history and culture.

In 160 BC, the Seleucid Empire, under the rule of King Demetrius I, was facing a rebellion led by Timarchus in the east. In response, Demetrius left his general, Bacchides, in charge of the western part of the empire and tasked him with maintaining control of the province of Judea. Bacchides led an army into Judea on a second expedition, following a previous visit in late 162/early 161 BC. The Seleucid army carried out a massacre of Jews in the Galilee and marched south towards Jerusalem. This tactic was intended to force Judas Maccabeus, the leader of the Jewish rebellion, to engage in open battle and protect his reputation, as well as weaken the faction of Alcimus, who claimed to be better able to protect the people from future killings. Bacchides then took a route towards Jerusalem that likely surprised the Maccabees: the arduous route through Mount Beth El, which required climbing an arid mesa. The Seleucids, possibly with an element of surprise, approached the area of Berea, just south of Beth El, to set up their camp. A mere kilometer away, Judas and the Maccabee army were camped at Elasa. Bacchides' army was recorded as having 20,000 infantry and 2,000 cavalry, while the size of the rebel army is disputed. Some sources, such as 1 Maccabees, claim that Judas's army at Elasa was small, with only 3,000 men of which 800 or 1,000 would actually fight. However, historians suspect the true numbers were larger, possibly as many as 22,000 soldiers, and the author may have downplayed their strength in an attempt to explain the defeat.

The Battle

The Battle of Elasa was fought on the plateau between Elasa and Berea. The terrain there was not perfectly flat, but its slope was open and gentle enough to allow for the use of phalanx tactics, which likely favored the experienced Seleucid heavy infantry. In order to gain an advantage, the Seleucids deployed their cavalry on the flanks, with a heavy infantry phalanx in the center and skirmishers, including archers and slingers, in front. Bacchides himself commanded from the elite cavalry on the right flank, as was custom in Hellenistic armies. Judas Maccabeus, on the other hand, opted to attack the right flank of the Seleucid army with the hope of killing the commander, similar to his victory over Nicanor at the Battle of Adasa. The loss of a commander could have caused the Seleucids to retreat and rattled the entire army.

The elite horsemen on the right retreated from the Jewish advance and the Maccabees pursued, possibly as far as Baal-hazor (modern Tall Asur) at the foot of the Judaean Mountains. The battle is described as lasting from "morning until evening," suggesting that the pursuit by Judas's force after Bacchides may have lasted some time. This retreat may have been a tactic from Bacchides, however, to feign weakness and draw the Maccabees in where they could be surrounded and defeated, with their own retreat cut off. Regardless of whether it was intentional or not, the Seleucids regained their formation and trapped the rebel army with their own left flank of cavalry, which circled around to cut off Judas's escape. Judas was eventually killed and the remaining Judeans fled. Despite the loss, the rebels were somehow able to recover Judas's body afterward, unlike Eleazar's body after his death. The account in 1 Maccabees reports that Judas's brothers Jonathan and Simon accomplished the deed, while Josephus reports it was thanks to an agreement with Bacchides afterward. 1 Maccabees concludes with a lament for Judas, quoting King David's lament over the death of King Saul: "How the mighty have fallen!"

It is important to note that this battle was a significant setback for the Maccabees, losing their leader Judas Maccabeus and the battle itself. However, the Maccabees continued the rebellion, and under the leadership of Judas' brothers, Jonathan and Simon, they were able to establish an independent Jewish state known as the Hasmonean Kingdom.

Aftermath

The aftermath of the Battle of Elasa saw the Seleucid Empire reasserting their authority in Jerusalem and other major cities of Judea. Judas Maccabeus' brother, Jonathan Apphus, became the new leader of the Maccabees and continued to engage in skirmishes against Bacchides' troops. However, these skirmishes did not lead to significant gains for the Maccabees. Bacchides fortified the major cities of Judea and took hostages from prominent Jewish families as a guarantee of cooperation. He also garrisoned fortresses in Jericho, Emmaus, Beth-horon, Bethel, Timnath, Pharathon, and Tephon. The largest concentration of Greek troops remained at the Acra citadel in Jerusalem, Beth-zur, and Gazara.

The Hasmonean family suffered another loss when Judas and Jonathan's brother, John Gaddi, was sent to negotiate with the Nabateans, who had cooperated with the Maccabees in earlier years of the struggle, but was killed by the sons of Jambri, a family that had turned hostile to the Hasmoneans. Bacchides and Jonathan eventually came to a peace deal, but the Maccabees were reduced to their initial position at the start of the revolt in 167 BC: as a guerrilla movement based in the countryside. Bacchides returned to Syria in late 160 BC. Jonathan and his allies later attacked a wedding held by a member of Jambri's family, killing many of the attendees, to avenge the loss of his brother John.

It is important to note that, despite the setback of the Battle of Elasa, the Maccabean Revolt continued and ultimately led to the establishment of an independent Jewish state, the Hasmonean Kingdom, which was a significant achievement in Jewish history and culture. The Maccabees, who emerged as powerful leaders and military commanders, are remembered as heroes in Jewish tradition and celebrated in the Jewish festival of Hanukkah.

Analysis

The Battle of Elasa, fought between the Maccabees and the Seleucid Empire in 160 BC, has been the subject of much analysis by historians. Israeli historian Bezalel Bar-Kochva argues that the Judeans would have had equal numbers to the Seleucids in this battle, that Bacchides' retreat was feigned in order to lure Judas into a vulnerable position, and that the Seleucid phalanx managed to best the Judean phalanx in a full-scale battle. Bar-Kochva believes that the author of 1 Maccabees, who admired Judas greatly, gave Judas an excuse for losing the battle by dramatically downplaying the number of soldiers. However, he maintains that the sources indicate that Judas was a superb military commander, and a superb military commander would not have charged an army outnumbered 20:1 in open terrain.

Bar-Kochva also cites other battles of the Seleucid army in places other than Judea, where the Seleucids were adept at using stratagems such as feigned retreats to lure their enemies into difficult positions, as well as other battles in uneven terrain in which the Seleucid phalanx acquitted itself well. Additionally, he notes that while 1 Maccabees gives little information on the composition of the Judean army, various "slips of the pen" suggest that the Jews themselves had their own cavalry and phalanxes.

1 Maccabees records a poetic lament for Judas as he sees his army slipping away. As with Judas's other pre-battle speeches and prayers in the book, this is best seen as a free composition by the author, not an actual transcription of Judas's words, in the style of Hellenistic historians to invent such dialogue to be more literary. One part of the speech also seemingly does not match Judas's other actions.

The Seleucid army is described as having slingers among its vanguard, which is unusual but not considered implausible. The sling was not generally a style that Syrian Greeks themselves trained in, but locals from Coele-Syria did, if used as auxiliaries, as could mercenaries from various nearby regions.

Fictional Story of the Battle of Elasa

As the sun rose on the barren plateau of Elasa, the Judean rebels, led by the fierce and determined Judas Maccabeus, prepared for battle. They had been tracking the Seleucid army for days, led by the ruthless general Bacchides, and they knew that this was their chance to strike a decisive blow against the oppressors of their people.

Judas rallied his troops, a ragtag band of farmers and shepherds, and reminded them of their cause. "We are fighting for our freedom, for our families, for our very way of life," he shouted. "We will not be cowed by the might of the Seleucids. We will not be defeated!"

The Seleucids, with their well-trained and heavily armed soldiers, marched towards the rebel camp, their banners flying high. But Judas and his men were not afraid. They had been fighting for years, and they knew that they had the support of the people and the favor of the gods.

As the two armies clashed, the sound of swords ringing and arrows whistling filled the air. The Seleucid phalanx, with its heavy infantry, pushed forward, but the Judeans held their ground, fighting with all their might.

Judas himself led the charge against Bacchides, hoping to strike a fatal blow to the Seleucid commander. But Bacchides was a shrewd and cunning warrior, and he had a trick up his sleeve. He feigned a retreat, drawing the Judeans in and surrounding them. The Seleucid cavalry closed in, cutting off any hope of escape.

But Judas and his men fought on, determined to the last. They knew that they were outmatched, but they would not give up without a fight. And as the sun began to set, the Judeans were finally defeated, but not before they had inflicted heavy casualties on the Seleucids.

As the dust settled, Judas lay on the battlefield, his wounds fatal. His brothers, Jonathan and Simon, rushed to his side and vowed to avenge his death and continue the fight for freedom. The Seleucids may have won the battle, but the war was far from over.

The Seleucids were able to reassert their authority in Jerusalem and the other major cities of Judea, but the Maccabees continued to skirmish against Bacchides' troops. The Maccabees were reduced to their initial position at the start of the revolt in 167 BC: as a guerrilla movement based in the countryside. Bacchides returned to Syria in late 160 BC.

But the Maccabean Revolt continued, and ultimately led to the establishment of an independent Jewish state, the Hasmonean Kingdom, which was a significant achievement in Jewish history and culture. The Maccabees, who emerged as powerful leaders and military commanders, are remembered as heroes in Jewish tradition and celebrated in the Jewish festival of Hanukkah. The memory of Judas Maccabeus, who fought and died for the freedom and independence of his people, would live on forever.

CHAPTER 14 1 Book of Maccabees Assessed

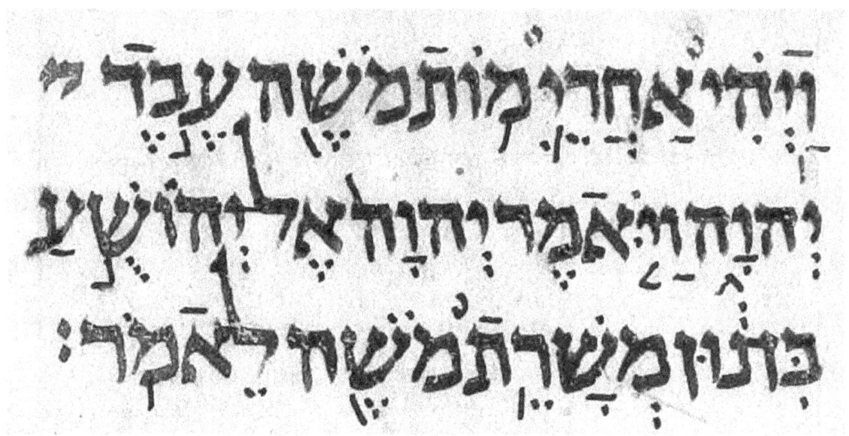

Image 25 Aleppo Codex Joshua 1:1

The First Book of Maccabees also referred to as 1 Maccabees, is a historical text that was written in Hebrew by an anonymous Jewish author after the establishment of an independent Jewish kingdom by the Hasmonean dynasty in the late 2nd century BC. The original Hebrew version of the text is no longer in existence, and the most significant surviving version is the Greek translation found in the Septuagint. While 1 Maccabees is considered to be canonical scripture by certain Christian denominations such as the Catholic, Orthodox, and Oriental Orthodox churches, it is not recognized as scripture by Protestant denominations or any major branches of Judaism. Some Protestants consider it to be an apocryphal book, which are texts that are not considered to be part of the official canon of scripture. The book is most well-known for its account of an early victory in the Maccabean Revolt against the Seleucid Empire, specifically the recapture of Jerusalem in 164 BC and the rededication of the Second Temple, which is the narrative behind the Jewish holiday of Hanukkah.

Name Maccabees

The name Maccabee is derived from the Hebrew word for "Hammer" and was first applied to the leader of the Maccabean Revolt, Judas Maccabeus, who was the third son of Mattathias. The origins of the surname "Maccabee" are uncertain, and there are several explanations for its meaning. One theory is that the name comes from the Aramaic word "maqqaba," which means "hammer" or "sledgehammer," in reference to Judas' ferocity in battle. Another explanation is that the name refers to his weapon of choice. According to Jewish folklore, the name Maccabee is an acronym for the phrase "Mi kamokha ba'elim Adonai," meaning "Who among the gods is like you, O Adonai?" which was the battle-cry of the Maccabees. Some scholars believe that the name is a shortened form of the Hebrew phrase "maqqab-Yahu," meaning "the one designated by Yahweh." While the surname Maccabee was initially only associated with Judas, it later came to represent all of the Hasmoneans who participated in the Maccabean Revolt.

Literary Form In 1 Maccabees

The literary form of the First Book of Maccabees is primarily prose, but it also includes several poetic sections that are written in the style of classical Hebrew poetry. These poetic interludes include four laments and three hymns of praise, which serve to add emotional depth and richness to the narrative. The book is divided into 16 chapters. Some widely used English translations of the Bible that include 1 Maccabees are the New Revised Standard Version (NRSV), Good News Translation (GNT), New American Bible, Revised Edition (NABRE), and the Knox Bible. These translations provide readers with different interpretations but ultimately aim to convey the historical and religious significance of the text.

Date of 1 Maccabees

The estimated date of the composition of the First Book of Maccabees is a topic of scholarly debate, with most scholars agreeing that it was written around 100 BC. The Jerusalem Bible suggests that it was written before the capture of Jerusalem by the Roman general Pompey in 63 BC. This date is supported by a number of factors, including historical references and literary style. However, it should be noted that the exact date of the book's composition is uncertain and some scholars argue for slightly different dates. Nevertheless, the consensus among scholars is that the book was written in the late 2nd century BC, before the Roman conquest of Jerusalem.

Contents of 1 Maccabees

Structure

The contents of the First Book of Maccabees are divided into several sections that are structured to provide a chronological account of the Maccabean Revolt. The Jerusalem Bible, for instance, breaks the book into five sections:

- The first chapter serves as an introduction and sets the stage for the events that follow.

- The second chapter focuses on Mattathias and the Holy War.

- The third to ninth chapters cover the period of the rebellion under the leadership of Judas Maccabeus.

- The tenth to twelfth chapters cover the period of the rebellion under the leadership of Jonathan.

- The final chapters, thirteen to sixteen, cover the period of the rebellion under the leadership of Simon. Each of these sections provides a detailed account of the events that occurred during the Maccabean Revolt, including the key figures, battles, and events that shaped the rebellion and its eventual outcome.

Detailed Summary

The First Book of Maccabees is a historical text that details the events of the Maccabean Revolt, a rebellion of the Jewish people against the Greek Seleucid Empire in the 2nd century BC. The setting of the book is about a century and a half after the conquest of Judea by the Greeks under Alexander the Great, and it covers the period from 175 to 134 BC. The book tells the story of how the Greek ruler Antiochus IV Epiphanes attempted to suppress the practice of basic Jewish law, resulting in the Maccabean Revolt. The rebellion was led by Mattathias and his family, particularly his sons Judas Maccabeus, Jonathan Apphus, and Simon Thassi and Simon's son John Hyrcanus. The book reflects traditional Jewish teaching, and it also provides a list of Jewish colonies scattered throughout the Mediterranean at the time.

The book begins by describing the conquest of Judea by Alexander the Great, and the subsequent rule of the Seleucid king Antiochus IV Epiphanes. Antiochus invades Jerusalem, removes sacred objects from the Temple, and imposes a tax and a fortress in the city. He then attempts to suppress Jewish laws and customs, and even desecrates the Temple by setting up pagan rituals. He also forbids circumcision, possession of Jewish scriptures, observance of the Sabbath, and offering of sacrifices at the Temple, and requires Jewish leaders to sacrifice to idols.

The narrative then introduces Mattathias and his five sons, a priestly family who live in Modein. Mattathias calls upon people loyal to the traditions of Israel to oppose the invaders and the Jewish Hellenizers, and his sons begin a military campaign against them (the Maccabean Revolt). The narrative reports different wars involving Judas and his brothers, Simon and Jonathan. In 165 BC, the Temple is freed and reconsecrated, so that ritual sacrifices may begin again. The festival of Hanukkah is instituted by Judas Maccabeus and his brothers to celebrate this event. The book also reports an alliance between the Jewish nation and the Roman Republic, aiming to remove the Greeks. The book ends with the death of Simon and the accession of his son John Hyrcanus.

The Canonicity of 1 Maccabees

The canonicity of the First Book of Maccabees refers to its acceptance as part of the biblical canon, or the official collection of sacred texts, by certain religious denominations. The book is considered to be canonical scripture by the Catholic, Orthodox, and Oriental Orthodox churches, as it is included in their list of accepted texts. This canonicity was established at several historical councils, including Pope Damasus I's Council of Rome in 382, if the Decretum Gelasianum is correctly associated with it, Origen of Alexandria (253), Augustine of Hippo (c. 397 AD), Pope Innocent I (405), Synod of Hippo (393), the Council of Carthage (397), the Council of Carthage (419), the Apostolic Canons, the Council of Florence (1442) and the Council of Trent (1546) listed the first two books of Maccabees as canonical. However, it is not considered to be part of the canon by Protestant denominations or any major branches of Judaism.

Transmission, Language and Author

The First Book of Maccabees is a historical text that is part of the Septuagint, a collection of Jewish texts translated into Greek. The text is extant in three codices of the Koine Greek Septuagint: the Codex Sinaiticus, Codex Alexandrinus, and Codex Vaticanus, as well as some cursives. The original book is speculated to have been written in Hebrew, due to a number of Hebrew idioms in the text, but if so, the Hebrew version has been lost, and the only extant version is found in the Septuagint. The date of the original Hebrew text is uncertain, with some authors dating it closer to the events it covers, while others suggest a later date. The author is unknown, but it is believed to have been written early in the reign of the Hasmoneans, likely during the rule of John Hyrcanus. The author has detailed knowledge of the geography of Judea and the broader Land of Israel and the events of the Maccabean Revolt. The author's purpose is to promote the view that the Hasmoneans were God's chosen and rightful rulers, and to present the events of the revolt as divinely ordained. The author also seeks to justify the Hasmonean's claim to rule by equating their deeds with heroes of the Hebrew Bible and by criticizing internal Jewish opponents of the Hasmoneans.

CHAPTER 15 2 Book of Maccabees Assessed

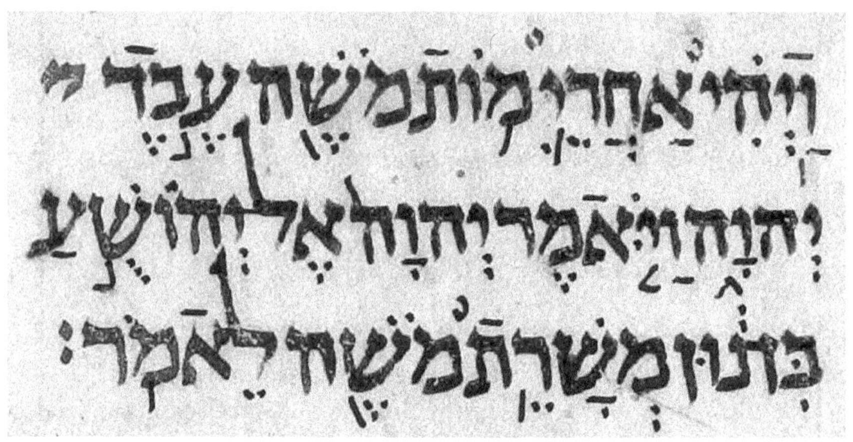

2 Maccabees, also known as the Second Book of Maccabees, is a book that is not included in the traditional canon of the Hebrew Bible but is considered part of the Septuagint and the Catholic and Orthodox Christian Old Testament. It is a historical account of the persecution of Jews under the rule of King Antiochus IV Epiphanes and the subsequent Maccabean Revolt, led by Judas Maccabeus, against the Seleucid Empire. The book concludes with the defeat of the Seleucid Empire general Nicanor in 161 BC by Judas Maccabeus. It was written in Koine Greek by a Jewish author living in Egypt, likely between 150 and 120 BC. It is considered to be an important source of information on the Maccabean Revolt, and it is not a continuation of 1 Maccabees but its own independent rendering of the historical events. The book starts with an incident in 178 BC when the Seleucid official Heliodorus attempted to tax the Second Temple and ends with the Battle of Adasa in 161 BC. Some scholars believe that the book may have been influenced by the Pharisaic tradition, which includes an endorsement of prayer for the dead and a belief in the resurrection of the dead.

2 Maccabees is a book that was included in the Septuagint, a Greek collection of Jewish scripture, but was not immediately translated into

Hebrew or included in the Masoretic Hebrew canon, known as the Tanakh. While it may have been read by Greek-speaking Jews in the centuries following its creation, later Jews did not consider the work to be of canonical or significant importance. However, early Christians did hold the work in high regard, and it was included as a deuterocanonical work of the Old Testament. Today, Catholic, Eastern Orthodox, and Oriental Orthodox Christians still recognize 2 Maccabees as deuterocanonical, however, Protestant Christians do not consider it to be part of the canon, although it is often included as part of the biblical apocrypha, which are noncanonical books that are still considered useful for education.

Authorship and Composition Date

The author of 2 Maccabees is not known, but the book claims to be an abridgment of a five-volume work by a man named Jason of Cyrene. The original work by Jason is not preserved and it is uncertain how much of the present text of 2 Maccabees is derived from his writing. The book was written in Greek, and there is no evidence of an earlier Hebrew version. Some sections, such as the Preface, Epilogue, and some reflections on morality, are believed to have been added by the author and not by Jason.

Scholars disagree on when Jason's original work was written and when 2 Maccabees was composed. Some argue that Jason's work was written around 160-140 BC, during the time of the Maccabean Revolt, while others suggest it could have been written at any point before 2 Maccabees. The dating of 2 Maccabees is also a subject of debate among scholars, with suggestions ranging from 150-100 BC. It is generally agreed that the work must have been written no later than the 70s BC, as the author does not appear to be aware of the Roman conquest of Judea under Pompey in 63 BC. The work may have undergone some modifications after its initial creation, but the version that is included in the Septuagint, the Greek Jewish scripture, is considered its final form. The Septuagint version also gave the work its title of "2 Maccabees" to distinguish it from other books in the collection. The original title of the work, if it had one, is unknown.

The author is believed to be an Egyptian Jew, possibly writing from Alexandria, addressing other Jews in the diaspora. The Greek style of the writer is considered to be educated and scholarly, and he is familiar with the forms of rhetoric and argument of the era. The book includes two letters sent by Jews in Jerusalem to Jews in Hellenistic Egypt concerning the feast days established to celebrate the purification of the temple (Hanukkah) and the defeat of Nicanor. If the author of the book inserted these letters, the book would have to have been written after 188 SE (~124 BC), the date of the second letter. Some scholars believe these letters were a later addition, while others consider them to be the foundation of the work.

Structure of 2 Maccabees

2 Maccabees is divided into 15 chapters, and each chapter covers a different aspect of the history surrounding the Maccabean Revolt.

1:1-2:18: The book begins with two letters sent by Jews in Jerusalem to Jews of the diaspora in Hellenistic Egypt concerning the feast day established to celebrate the purification of the temple (Hanukkah) and the feast to celebrate the defeat of Nicanor.

2:19-32: The preface of the Epitomist, which is the author of the abridged version of the work.

3: Heliodorus, a Seleucid official, attempts to tax the Temple in Jerusalem's treasury but is repelled. (178 BC)

4: The high priest Onias III of the Temple in Jerusalem is succeeded by his brother Jason, who is then succeeded by the corrupt Menelaus. Onias III is murdered. (175-170 BC)

5: Jason attempts to overthrow Menelaus. King Antiochus IV Epiphanes returns from his second expedition of the Sixth Syrian War in Egypt, defeats Jason's supporters, sacks Jerusalem, loots the Temple treasury, and kills and enslaves local Jews as retribution for the perceived revolt. Jason is forced into exile. (168 BC)

6: The Temple is converted into a syncretic Greek-Jewish worship site. Antiochus IV issues decrees forbidding traditional Jewish practices, such as circumcision, keeping kosher, and keeping the Sabbath. Eleazar the scribe is tortured and killed after refusing to eat pork. (168-167 BC)

7: Martyrdom of the woman and her seven sons after torture by Antiochus IV.

8: Start of the Maccabean Revolt. Judas Maccabeus defeats Nicanor, Gorgias, and Ptolemy son of Dorymenes at the Battle of Emmaus. (166-165 BC)

9:1-10:9: Antiochus IV is stricken with disease by God. He belatedly repents and writes a letter attempting to make peace before dying in Persia. Judas conquers Jerusalem, cleanses the Temple, and establishes the festival of Hanukkah. (164 BC)

10:10-38: Lysias becomes regent. Governor Ptolemy Macron attempts to cement peace with the Jews, but is undermined by anti-Jewish nobles and commits suicide. The Maccabees campaign in outlying regions against Timothy of Ammon and others. (163 BC)

11: Lysias leads a military expedition to Judea. Judas defeats him at the Battle of Beth Zur. Four documents detailing negotiations with Lysias and the Roman Republic. (160s BC)

12: More accounts of the campaigns in outlying regions against Timothy, Gorgias, and others. (163 BC)

13: Lysias orders the execution of unpopular High Priest Menelaus. Judas harries Lysias's expedition with minor victories. Lysias leaves and returns to the capital of Antioch to face the usurper Philip. (163-162 BC, likely near in time to the Battle of Beth Zechariah described in 1 Maccabees)

14:1-15:36: Demetrius I becomes King. Alcimus, who had replaced Menelaus as High Priest, is affirmed by Demetrius I. Nicanor is appointed governor of Judea. Nicanor and Judas enter negotiations for peace, but are subverted by Alcimus, who complains to the king; Judas's arrest is ordered. Nicanor threatens to destroy the Temple. In a dream vision, Onias III and the prophet Jeremiah give Judas a divine golden sword. At the Battle of Adasa, Judas defeats and kills Nicanor, preserving the sanctity of the Temple. The Day of Nicanor festival is established. (161 BC)

15:37-39: The Epitomist's

Contents of 2 Maccabees

2 Maccabees covers a period of history that predates that of 1 Maccabees, specifically focusing on the time period between the high priest Onias III and King Seleucus IV in 180 BC to the defeat of Nicanor in 161 BC. The exact focus of the work is a subject of debate among scholars. Most agree that the work has a moralistic tone, highlighting the triumph of Judaism, the supremacy of God, and the just punishment of those who oppose it. Some scholars view the book as a tribute to Judas Maccabeus, depicting the background of the Revolt as a means of praising him; others see the focus as being on the Second Temple and how it was gradually corrupted by Antiochus IV and how it was saved and purified; others see the focus as being on the city of Jerusalem and how it was saved; and others disagree with all of these interpretations, seeing the book as written solely for literary and entertainment purposes.

The author of 2 Maccabees is interested in providing a theological interpretation of the events, with God's interventions being seen as directing the course of events, punishing the wicked and restoring the Temple to his people. Some events are presented out of chronological order to make theological points, such as the occasional "flash forward" to a villain's later death. The numbers cited for the sizes of armies may also appear exaggerated, but this varies depending on the manuscript.

After the introductory stories of the controversies at the Temple and the persecutions of Antiochus IV, the narrative shifts to the Revolt itself. Following the death of Antiochus IV Epiphanes, the Feast of the Dedication of the Temple is established. The newly dedicated Temple is then threatened by the Seleucid general Nicanor. After his death, the festivities for the dedication are concluded, and a special day is dedicated to commemorate the Jewish victory in the month of Adar, on the day before "Mordecai's Day" (Purim). The book explicitly urges diaspora Jews to celebrate both Hanukkah and Nicanor's Day.

The Canonicity of 2 Maccabees

2 Maccabees is considered a deuterocanonical book by Catholic, Eastern Orthodox, and Oriental Orthodox Christians, meaning that it is considered part of the canon of scripture but is not considered to be on the same level of authority as the protocanonical books. Protestants, on the other hand, do not regard 2 Maccabees as canonical, although many include it as part of the biblical apocrypha, which are non-canonical books considered useful for the purpose of edification.

The theology of 2 Maccabees is heavily focused on God's intervention in the affairs of his people. The book portrays God as actively punishing the wicked and restoring the Temple to his people. The events presented in the book are often presented with a moralistic tone, showing the triumph of Judaism, the supremacy of God, and the just punishment of villains. The author also emphasizes the importance of Hanukkah and the feast to celebrate the defeat of Nicanor, which are festivals that are established in the book.

Hellenistic Judaism

2 Maccabees was written with a specific audience in mind, the Greek-speaking Jews of the diaspora. The book was included in the Septuagint, a Greek collection of Jewish scripture that was used by Greek-speaking Jews and early Christians. However, 2 Maccabees was not translated to Hebrew nor included in the Masoretic Hebrew canon, the Tanakh, which was the canon used by Jews who kept to the Hebrew version of the Jewish Scriptures. As a result, 2 Maccabees did not become part of the Jewish canon, and was not widely read or regarded as important by later Jews.

The work is set within the context of Hellenistic Judaism, a form of Judaism that emerged during the Hellenistic period, characterized by the fusion of Jewish and Greek cultures, and the adoption of Greek language and culture by Jews. Many of the Jews in the diaspora, particularly in Egypt, were heavily influenced by Greek culture, and the author of 2 Maccabees addresses this audience, providing a theological interpretation of the events of the Maccabean Revolt that emphasizes the role of God in the affairs of his people.

Scholars have debated the possible influences on the author of 2 Maccabees, with some suggesting that the author might have been influenced by the Pharisaic tradition. The Pharisees were a Jewish sect that emphasized adherence to Jewish law and disputed with the rulers of the Hasmonean kingdom, the dynasty that emerged after the Maccabean Revolt. They criticized the Hasmoneans for taking on both the role of Chief Priest and King, and called for them to cede one of the titles. Some scholars have suggested that the author of 2 Maccabees, who praises Judas Maccabeus for saving the Temple, might have been a Pharisee from Judea who wrote the book while in Egyptian exile. However, other scholars disagree with this theory and believe that the author does not show any signs of Pharisaic inclinations.

The theology of the work, which emphasizes the resurrection of the dead, is an update to the "Deuteronomist" history seen in older Jewish works. The classical Deuteronomist view was that when Israel was faithful to the covenant, the Jews prospered, and when Israel neglected the covenant, God withdrew his favor and Israel suffered. The author of 2 Maccabees tries to make sense of the fact that the most faithful Jews suffered the most during the persecution of Antiochus IV, by explaining that the suffering was a swift and merciful corrective to set the Jews back on the right path. He also emphasizes the idea that post-mortem rewards and punishments would accomplish what might have been lacking in the mortal world. These references to the resurrection of the dead would prove especially influential among Roman-era Jews who converted to Christianity.

Image 26 A Byzantine-style fresco at the Santa Maria Antiqua church in Rome, likely painted around 650 AD. It depicts the woman and her seven sons (here named Solomne) and Eleazar, their teacher. The story of their martyrdom is the most famous part of 2 Maccabee

Christianity in the Era of the Roman Empire

2 Maccabees, like 1 Maccabees, was considered a deuterocanonical book by early Christians, meaning it was considered to be a secondary canon of scripture but still held value for edification and teaching. The Septuagint, a Greek collection of Jewish scripture, included 2 Maccabees and it was used as the basis for the Old Testament in early Christianity. However, not all Christian denominations consider it canonical and it is not included in the Masoretic Hebrew canon, the Tanakh.

The Catholic, Eastern Orthodox and Oriental Orthodox Christians still consider 2 Maccabees to be deuterocanonical, while Protestant Christians do not regard it as canonical. However, many Protestant Christians still consider it a part of the biblical apocrypha, which are noncanonical books that are useful for teaching and edification.

Theologically, 2 Maccabees resonated with early Christians due to its stories of martyrology and the resurrection of the dead. Christians drew comparisons between the Maccabean martyrs and Christian martyrs, and the book's emphasis on upholding the Jewish Law and the promise of an eventual salvation also resonated with early Christians. However, there were also awkward aspects in the book such as the martyrs dying to uphold Jewish Law in an era when many Christians felt that the Law of Moses was obsolete. Christian authors generally downplayed the Jewishness of the martyrs and treated them as proto-Christians instead.

Controversy in the Reformation Era

During the Reformation era of the 1500s, 2 Maccabees was considered an official part of the canon, but as a deuterocanonical work, it was seen as less important than the older scriptures. However, some Catholic authors, such as Josse van Clichtove, cited 2 Maccabees as support for the idea of dead saints interceding for the salvation of the living and for prayers for the dead, which was the idea of the souls in purgatory. Martin Luther and other reformers, like Jean Calvin, had objections to the book and its use in support of the Catholic doctrine of purgatory and the idea of the intercession of saints, which they disagreed with. Luther wished for a strict canon and preferred the Hebrew Bible as the basis for the Old Testament. Calvin felt that salvation was strictly God's choice and not something that dead saints could intervene on. In response to this, the Catholic Church affirmed at the Council of Trent in 1546 that 2 Maccabees (and other deuterocanonical works) were fully reliable as scripture.

⸿ O mynsch beschauwe diß sacramentlige figur Marie
yrs kyndes Jesu/ Salomoen yrer seuē kynd zofur erledit

Image 27 A 1517 German depiction of the crucified Jesus, the mother, and her seven sons in the boiling cauldron.

Literary Influence

2 Maccabees has had a significant literary influence throughout history, particularly in its stories of the martyrdom of Eleazar and the woman with seven sons. One of the most notable examples is the book of 4 Maccabees, written by a 1st-century Jewish author who used 2 Maccabees as a direct source. 4 Maccabees expands on the martyrdoms described in 2 Maccabees but provides a different interpretation of them. The author of 4 Maccabees, who was schooled in Stoic philosophy, presents the martyred woman and Eleazar as calmly discussing matters with their oppressors, using reason and intellectual argument to stay calm and defy Antiochus IV. It also takes the idea of the resurrection of the dead even more directly than 2 Maccabees and the Book of Daniel. Another work, 3 Maccabees, also evinces familiarity with 2 Maccabees. The Christian Epistle to the Hebrews may also make a reference to 2 Maccabees. A later work that directly expanded 2 Maccabees was the Yosippon of the 10th century, which includes a paraphrase of parts of the Latin translation of 2 Maccabees. Despite this, among Jews, there had been practically no interest in 2 Maccabees itself for a millennium, and the Yosippon was a rare exception of medieval Jews rediscovering the work. The story of the mother and her seven sons remained the most retold and influential in all the works.

Reliability as History

2 Maccabees is traditionally viewed as a less reliable source of historical information about the Maccabean Revolt than 1 Maccabees by secular historians, particularly in the 19th century. This is due to several factors, such as its overt religious moralizing, its tendency to jump around in time and place, and the inclusion of implausible claims that conflict with information in 1 Maccabees. Most scholars consider 1 Maccabees to be a more accurate source of information about the military aspects of the revolt, as it was written by a Judean who accurately names and describes locations, provides more detail on maneuvers and tactics, and has more realistic figures for things like troop counts and casualties. Additionally, 2 Maccabees is written in a

style that is meant to appeal to emotions and sentiment, which skeptical historians believe suggests that the author was more interested in telling a good story than in historical accuracy.

In the 20th century, scholars began to re-evaluate the historical reliability of 2 Maccabees as a source on the Maccabean Revolt. Previously, it was considered to be a less reliable source than 1 Maccabees due to its religious bias and lack of chronological order. However, scholars recognized that a politically-slanted history, such as 1 Maccabees, can also be unreliable. They came to the conclusion that the historical documents present in 2 Maccabees, while seemingly out of order, were likely legitimate and matched what would be expected of Seleucid negotiations. Archaeological evidence supported many of the references made to Seleucid leadership, leading historians to believe that the author of 2 Maccabees had better knowledge of internal Seleucid affairs than the author of 1 Maccabees. For example, 2 Maccabees appears to be more reliable in its account of the date of Antiochus IV's death and the targeting of his decrees against Judea and Samaria, rather than the empire as a whole as 1 Maccabees suggests.

In recent times, scholars have started to view 2 Maccabees as a valuable historical source, despite its religious bias. This is because it provides an independent account of the Maccabean Revolt, a rare occurrence in historical records. In the past, 2 Maccabees was considered a less reliable source than 1 Maccabees, mainly because of its religious moralizing, lack of chronological order and implausible claims. However, in the 20th century, historians began to acknowledge that a politically slanted history, such as 1 Maccabees, can be just as biased and unreliable as the religiously slanted history in 2 Maccabees. Furthermore, archaeological evidence supports many of the references made to Seleucid leadership in 2 Maccabees, suggesting that the author had access to internal Seleucid affairs. This, along with the fact that it is an independent source, makes 2 Maccabees an important historical document for understanding the Maccabean Revolt.

Manuscripts

2 Maccabees is a book that was included in some early manuscripts of the Septuagint, which is the Greek translation of the Hebrew Bible. However, the inclusion of 2 Maccabees in these manuscripts was not consistent. For example, the 5th century Codex Alexandrinus includes 2 Maccabees along with 1, 3, and 4 Maccabees, while the Codex Vaticanus and Codex Sinaiticus do not include 2 Maccabees. Additionally, ancient fragments of the text have been found, but some of these have been attributed to Lucian of Antioch, who is believed to have added or changed parts of the text, resulting in variations in the readings. A critical edition of the Greek text of 2 Maccabees was created by Robert Hanhart in 1959, with a second edition published in 1976.

CHAPTER 16 Jonathan Apphus (Maccabee)

Jonathan Apphus (also known as Jonathan Maccabee) was one of the sons of Mattathias, the Jewish priest who is credited with sparking the Maccabean Revolt against the Seleucid Empire. Jonathan was a prominent leader of the Hasmonean dynasty and played a key role in the establishment of Jewish independence in the 2nd century BC.

Background and Early Life

Jonathan was born in the early 160s BC in the village of Modiin, located in the central highlands of Judaea. He was the third son of Mattathias, a Jewish priest who became the leader of the rebellion against the Seleucid Empire. The Seleucids, who had taken control of the region following the death of Alexander the Great, sought to impose Hellenistic culture and religion on the Jewish population. This included the construction of Greek temples and the suppression of traditional Jewish practices.

Mattathias and his five sons, including Jonathan, were among the first to take up arms against the Seleucid forces. They became known as the Maccabees, a name that is thought to be derived from the Hebrew word for "hammer."

Military Leadership

Jonathan played a key role in the military campaign against the Seleucids. He led many successful battles and was able to expand the territory controlled by the Hasmonean dynasty. He was particularly successful in his attacks on the Seleucid garrisons and was able to capture many cities and towns in Judaea.

One of Jonathan's most notable victories was the Battle of Beth-Zeitim, where he was able to defeat a much larger Seleucid army. This was a turning point in the war, as it gave the Hasmoneans control of Jerusalem and the Temple.

Political Leadership

Jonathan was not only a skilled military leader, but also a savvy politician. He was able to secure alliances with other Jewish factions and with the Roman Republic. He also made alliances with neighboring countries such as Egypt and was able to secure the release of Jewish prisoners.

Jonathan also played a key role in the establishment of Jewish independence. He was able to negotiate with the Seleucid king, Demetrius I Soter, and was able to secure the recognition of Jewish autonomy in Judaea.

Death and Legacy

Jonathan was assassinated in 143 BC, by Trypho, a Seleucid general who had taken control of the empire after Demetrius I Soter was captured by the Parthians. He was buried in the city of Modiin, where he was born.

Jonathan's death did not end the Hasmonean dynasty, his brother Simon took over the leadership role and continued to strengthen the Jewish independence. Jonathan's leadership and military skills were instrumental in securing Jewish autonomy and his legacy is still remembered in Jewish history. The Hasmonean dynasty would continue to rule Judaea for more than a century, until the Roman Republic conquered the region in 63 BC.

CHAPTER 17 Simon Thassi (Maccabee)

Image 28 An imaginary depiction of Simon Thassi from Guillaume Rouillé's Promptuarii Iconum Insigniorum (1553)

Simon Thassi, also known as Simon Maccabee, was a prominent leader in the Jewish revolt against the Seleucid Empire in the 2nd century BC. He was the third son of Mattathias, the priest who initiated the rebellion, and he played a key role alongside his brothers, Judas

Maccabaeus and Jonathan Apphus, in leading the Jewish forces to victory against their Greek-Syrian oppressors.

Background

The Seleucid Empire, led by King Antiochus IV Epiphanes, had imposed strict laws on the Jewish people, including a ban on their religious practices and the desecration of their temple in Jerusalem. This oppression led to widespread anger and discontent among the Jewish population, and Mattathias, a priest from the village of Modiin, decided to take action. He and his five sons, including Simon, launched a rebellion against the Seleucid forces in 167 BC.

Role in the Revolt

Simon played a vital role in the Jewish rebellion against the Seleucids. He and his brothers Judas and Jonathan were able to rally the Jewish people and lead them in a series of successful military campaigns. Simon was known for his strategic thinking and his ability to inspire his troops. He was also a skilled diplomat, and he was able to negotiate alliances with neighboring kingdoms and tribes.

One of Simon's most notable achievements was his capture of the strategic city of Joppa, which gave the Jewish rebels control of the coast and access to the sea. He also played a key role in the reconsecration of the Temple in Jerusalem in 164 BC, an event that is still celebrated today as the holiday of Hanukkah.

After the Revolt

After the Jewish forces successfully defeated the Seleucids and regained control of Jerusalem, Simon and his brothers established the Hasmonean dynasty, which ruled over an independent Jewish kingdom for the next century. Simon was appointed as the ruler of the newly independent Jewish state and served as High Priest, a position of great religious and political power.

Simon's rule was marked by stability and prosperity, and he worked to improve the lives of his subjects by building infrastructure, promoting trade and commerce, and strengthening the Jewish state militarily. He also worked to solidify the Jewish identity of his kingdom by promoting the study of Torah and reinforcing Jewish laws and customs.

Simon Thassi's role in the Jewish revolt was crucial in leading the Jewish people to their independence and their right to practice their religion freely. He was a great leader, strategist, and diplomat and is remembered today as one of the most important figures in Jewish history.

CHAPTER 18 John Hyrcanus

Image 29 John Hyrcanus from Guillaume Rouillé's Promptuarii Iconum Insigniorum

John Hyrcanus, also known as Yochanan ben Matityahu, was a leader of the Hasmonean (Maccabean) dynasty and a Jewish high priest who ruled from 134 to 104 BC. He is considered one of the most significant figures in Jewish history, as his reign marked the beginning of the Hasmonean dynasty's rise to power and the emergence of an independent Jewish state.

Early Life and Rise to Power

John Hyrcanus was born into the Hasmonean family, a group of Jewish priests and warriors who had risen to prominence during the Maccabean Revolt against the Seleucid Empire in the 2nd century BC. He was the son of the Hasmonean leader, Mattathias, and the brother of Judas Maccabeus, who had led the revolt against the Seleucids.

After the death of Judas Maccabeus, his brother Jonathan succeeded him as leader of the Hasmoneans. John Hyrcanus served as Jonathan's military commander and was instrumental in consolidating Hasmonean control over Jerusalem and the surrounding areas.

When Jonathan was captured and executed by the Seleucid king Demetrius II in 143 BC, John Hyrcanus became the leader of the Hasmoneans. He immediately set about consolidating his power and expanding the territory under Hasmonean control.

Reign as High Priest and King

During his reign, John Hyrcanus continued to expand Hasmonean territory through a series of military campaigns. He conquered Idumea, a region south of Jerusalem, and forced the inhabitants to convert to Judaism. This brought a large number of new converts into the Jewish community and greatly expanded Hasmonean territory.

John Hyrcanus also strengthened the position of the Hasmoneans within the Jewish community by taking on the role of both high priest and king. This marked the beginning of the Hasmonean dynasty's rise to power as the ruling dynasty of the Jewish people.

John Hyrcanus was also known for his support of the Pharisees, a Jewish sect that emphasized strict adherence to Jewish law and the oral tradition. His support of the Pharisees helped to establish them as the dominant Jewish sect during his reign.

Economic and Cultural Development

Under John Hyrcanus, the Hasmonean kingdom experienced significant economic and cultural development. He built fortifications, roads and public works, and encouraged the growth of agriculture, particularly in the newly conquered territories.

He also promoted the spread of Jewish culture and religious practices. He supported the establishment of synagogues, and encouraged the translation of the Hebrew Bible into Greek so that it would be more accessible to the Jewish diaspora.

Legacy

John Hyrcanus is considered one of the most significant figures in Jewish history. His reign marked the beginning of the Hasmonean dynasty's rise to power and the emergence of an independent Jewish state. He expanded Hasmonean territory through military conquests, strengthened the position of the Hasmoneans within the Jewish community, and promoted economic and cultural development.

His support of the Pharisees helped to establish them as the dominant Jewish sect during his reign, and his encouragement of the translation of the Hebrew Bible into Greek had a lasting impact on Jewish culture and religion.

John Hyrcanus' legacy is still remembered in Jewish tradition and history, his reign is considered as one of the most important turning points in Jewish history, as it marked the beginning of an independent Jewish state and the rise of the Hasmonean dynasty as the ruling dynasty of the Jewish people.

CHAPTER 19 Aristobulus I

Image 30 Aristobulus I, woodcut designed by Guillaume Rouillé. From Promptuarii Iconum Insigniorum.

Aristobulus I, also known as Aristobulus ben John Hyrcanus, was the first Hasmonean king of Judaea, who ruled from 104 to 103 BC. He was a member of the Hasmonean dynasty, a group of Jewish priests and warriors who had risen to prominence during the Maccabean Revolt against the Seleucid Empire in the 2nd century BC.

Background and Rise to Power

Aristobulus was the eldest son of John Hyrcanus, the leader of the Hasmoneans and the Jewish high priest, who had ruled from 134 to 104 BC. After the death of his father, Aristobulus inherited the leadership of the Hasmoneans and the Jewish high priesthood.

Aristobulus was known for his ambition and desire for power. He saw the opportunity to expand the Hasmonean kingdom and sought to establish the Hasmonean dynasty as the ruling dynasty of the Jewish people.

Reign as King

Aristobulus' reign as king was marked by a series of conflicts and power struggles. He was faced with challenges from his brothers, who were also claimants to the Hasmonean throne and the high priesthood. In order to secure his power, Aristobulus resorted to violence and political intrigue.

One of his first acts as king was to assert his authority over the Jewish Sanhedrin, the highest judicial and legislative body in ancient Israel. He did this by exiling or killing his opponents and consolidating his control over the Sanhedrin.

Aristobulus also sought to expand the Hasmonean kingdom through military conquests. He led campaigns against the neighboring kingdoms of Iturea and Samaria, and was able to expand Hasmonean territory.

However, his reign was short-lived, as he was only able to rule for a year before he died in 103 BC.

Internal Conflicts

Aristobulus' reign was also marked by internal conflicts and power struggles within the Hasmonean family. His brothers, Alexander Jannaeus and Antigonus, also claimed the right to the Hasmonean throne and the high priesthood.

After his death, Alexander Jannaeus, who was also his brother, succeeded him as king and high priest, and was able to consolidate his power and rule for many years.

Legacy

Aristobulus I is considered an important figure in Jewish history as he was the first Hasmonean king of Judaea. His reign marked a significant turning point in Jewish history, as the Hasmonean dynasty established itself as the ruling dynasty of the Jewish people.

However, his reign was also marked by violence and political intrigue, as he sought to secure his power through the use of force and the elimination of his opponents.

His legacy is still remembered in Jewish tradition and history, his reign is considered as one of the most important turning points in Jewish history, as it marked the beginning of the Hasmonean dynasty's rule as the ruling dynasty of the Jewish people, and the first time that a member of the Hasmonean family has taken on the title of king.

It's worth noting that the reign of Aristobulus and the Hasmonean dynasty in general, was a period of political instability, constant power struggles, and conflicts between different factions within the Jewish community. The Hasmonean kings faced challenges from other Jewish sects and groups, and also from neighboring kingdoms and empires.

CHAPTER 20 Salome Alexandra

Image 31 Salome Alexandra, from Guillaume Rouillé's Promptuarii Iconum Insigniorum

Salome Alexandra, also known as Shlomtzion, was a Jewish queen who ruled as the last regnant queen of Judea and the last ruler of Judea to die as the sovereign of an independent kingdom. She was the wife of both Aristobulus I and Alexander Jannaeus, and played an important role in the politics and religious development of Judea during the 2nd century BC.

Background

Salome Alexandra was born into the Hasmonean dynasty, a Jewish priestly family that had gained political power in Judea during the 2nd century BC. She was the sister of Aristobulus I, who was the first Hasmonean ruler to assume the title of king.

Marriage to Aristobulus I

Salome Alexandra married Aristobulus I, and played a role in his rule as queen. However, Aristobulus I died shortly after his reign began, leaving Salome Alexandra a widow.

Marriage to Alexander Jannaeus

After the death of Aristobulus I, Salome Alexandra married his brother Alexander Jannaeus, who became the next king of Judea. Salome Alexandra's marriage to Alexander Jannaeus was politically motivated, as it helped to secure the Hasmonean dynasty's hold on the throne.

Rule as Queen

During her marriage to Alexander Jannaeus, Salome Alexandra played a significant role in the politics and religious development of Judea. She is credited with helping to reconcile the different Jewish sects that existed at the time and promoting religious tolerance. She was particularly supportive of the Pharisees, a Jewish sect that emphasized the study of the Torah and the adherence to traditional Jewish law.

Additionally, Salome Alexandra was known for her wisdom and her ability to make important decisions. She is said to have played a key role in the administration of the kingdom during her husband's reign.

Death and Legacy

Salome Alexandra died as the last regnant queen of Judea, and the last ruler of Judea to die as the sovereign of an independent kingdom. Her death marked the end of the Hasmonean dynasty's rule in Judea.

Salome Alexandra's reign is considered to be an important period in Jewish history. She helped to reconcile the different Jewish sects and promote religious tolerance, which helped to establish a sense of unity among the Jewish people. Additionally, her role as a powerful and influential queen in a male-dominated society is considered to be significant.

In conclusion, Salome Alexandra, also known as Shlomtzion, was a Jewish queen who played an important role in the politics and religious development of Judea during the 2nd century BC. She was the wife of both Aristobulus I and Alexander Jannaeus, and was the last regnant queen of Judea, and the last ruler of Judea to die as the sovereign of an independent kingdom. Her reign is considered to be an important period in Jewish history, and her role as a powerful and influential queen in a male-dominated society is considered to be significant.

CHAPTER 21 John Hyrcanus II

Image 32 Hyrcanus from Guillaume Rouillé's Promptuarii Iconum Insigniorum

John Hyrcanus II was a Jewish leader and member of the Hasmonean dynasty who served as the High Priest in the 1st century BC. He played a significant role in the politics and religious development of Judea during his time, and his reign was marked by internal conflict and struggles for power.

Background

John Hyrcanus II was born into the Hasmonean dynasty, a Jewish priestly family that had gained political power in Judea during the 2nd century BC. His father, Alexander Jannaeus, was the last ruler of the Hasmonean dynasty to die as the sovereign of an independent kingdom.

Accession to the High Priesthood

John Hyrcanus II inherited the High Priesthood from his father, Alexander Jannaeus, and served in this role for a long time during the 1st century BC. However, his tenure as High Priest was not without controversy, as he struggled for power with other members of the Hasmonean dynasty.

Internal Conflicts

During his time as High Priest, John Hyrcanus II was involved in a number of internal conflicts within the Hasmonean dynasty. He struggled for power with his brother, Aristobulus II, who also claimed the title of High Priest. These conflicts ultimately led to a civil war between the two brothers, with John Hyrcanus II ultimately emerging victorious.

Additionally, John Hyrcanus II was also involved in conflicts with other Jewish sects, such as the Pharisees and the Sadducees. These conflicts were largely centered around religious and political matters, and they further weakened the unity of the Jewish people.

Religious Reforms

Despite the internal conflicts and struggles for power, John Hyrcanus II made significant religious reforms during his time as High Priest. He is credited with establishing the practice of religious segregation, which required the separation of the Jewish people from their non-Jewish neighbors. This helped to strengthen the Jewish identity and promote adherence to Jewish law.

Additionally, John Hyrcanus II is also credited with expanding the Jewish territory during his time as High Priest. He conquered several neighboring territories, including Samaria and Idumea, and brought them under Jewish control.

Death and Legacy

John Hyrcanus II died as a High Priest, and his death marked the end of the Hasmonean dynasty's rule in Judea. His reign was marked by internal conflicts and struggles for power, and his religious reforms helped to strengthen the Jewish identity and promote adherence to Jewish law, but also created a divide among the Jewish sects.

Despite these challenges, John Hyrcanus II is remembered for his religious reforms and for his efforts to expand Jewish territory. His legacy continues to be studied and debated by scholars and historians, but his contributions and impact on Jewish history are undeniable.

In conclusion, John Hyrcanus II was a Jewish leader and member of the Hasmonean dynasty who served as the High Priest in the 1st century BC. He played a significant role in the politics and religious development of Judea during his time, and his reign was marked by internal conflict and struggles for power. Despite these challenges, John Hyrcanus II made significant religious reforms, helped to strengthen the Jewish identity and promote adherence to Jewish law and expanded Jewish territory. His legacy continues to be studied and debated by scholars and historians, but his contributions and impact on Jewish history are undeniable.

CHAPTER 22 Aristobulus II

Image 33 Aristobulus II, from Guillaume Rouillé's Promptuarii Iconum Insigniorum

Aristobulus II was a Jewish High Priest and King of Judea, who ruled from 66 BC to 63 BC, from the Hasmonean dynasty. He was a member of the Hasmonean dynasty, which had gained political power in Judea during the 2nd century BC, and he played a significant role in the politics and religious development of Judea during his time.

Background

Aristobulus II was born into the Hasmonean dynasty, a Jewish priestly family that had gained political power in Judea during the 2nd century BC. His father, Alexander Jannaeus, was the last ruler of the Hasmonean dynasty to die as the sovereign of an independent kingdom. He had a brother John Hyrcanus II, who was also a High Priest.

Accession to the High Priesthood and Kingship

Aristobulus II inherited the High Priesthood and Kingship from his father, Alexander Jannaeus, and served in these roles from 66 BC to 63 BC. His rule was marked by a struggle for power with his brother, John Hyrcanus II, who also claimed the title of High Priest and King.

Internal Conflicts

During his time as High Priest and King, Aristobulus II was involved in a number of internal conflicts within the Hasmonean dynasty. He struggled for power with his brother, John Hyrcanus II, who also claimed the title of High Priest and King. These conflicts ultimately led to a civil war between the two brothers, with Aristobulus II emerging victorious.

Additionally, Aristobulus II was also involved in conflicts with other Jewish sects, such as the Pharisees and the Sadducees. These conflicts were largely centered around religious and political matters, and they further weakened the unity of the Jewish people.

Religious Reforms

Despite the internal conflicts and struggles for power, Aristobulus II made significant religious reforms during his time as High Priest and King. He tried to strengthen the Jewish identity and promote adherence to Jewish law. He also supported the establishment of the

Sanhedrin, an assembly of Jewish religious leaders, which helped to provide a central authority for Jewish religious matters.

Political Decisions

Aristobulus II was also known for his political decisions, he was the first Hasmonean ruler to be crowned as King, this move was seen by some as a violation of traditional Jewish law, which did not permit the Hasmoneans to hold the throne. But he did not stop there, he also attempted to centralize the government and expand the borders of the Jewish state.

Capture and Death

Aristobulus II was captured by the Roman general Pompey in 63 BC and was exiled to Rome. He died in exile, and his death marked the end of the Hasmonean dynasty's rule in Judea. His reign was marked by internal conflicts and struggles for power, but his religious reforms and political decisions helped to strengthen the Jewish identity and promote adherence to Jewish law, but also created a divide among the Jewish sects.

In conclusion, Aristobulus II was a Jewish High Priest and King of Judea, who ruled from 66 BC to 63 BC, from the Hasmonean dynasty. He played a significant role in the politics and religious development of Judea during his time. His rule was marked by internal conflicts and struggles for power, but his religious reforms and political decisions helped to strengthen the Jewish identity and promote adherence to Jewish law, but also created a divide among the Jewish sects. He was the last Hasmonean ruler; his capture and death marked the end of the Hasmonean dynasty's rule in Judea.

CHAPTER 23 Sadducees, Jewish Religious Leaders

Image 34 The Pharisees and the Sadducees Come to Tempt Jesus by James Tissot (Brooklyn Museum)

The Sadducees were a Jewish sect that emerged in the Second Temple period. They were a powerful and influential group of religious leaders and played a significant role in Jewish politics and religion during the Second Temple period.

Background

The Sadducees were a Jewish sect that emerged in the Second Temple period, which lasted from 516 BCE to 70 CE. They were a powerful and influential group of religious leaders, who were primarily made up of the upper class and the aristocracy of Jewish society. They were known for their conservative interpretation of Jewish law and their strict adherence to the written Torah, which consists of the first five books of the Hebrew Bible.

Beliefs

The Sadducees believed in the strict adherence to the written Torah, which consists of the first five books of the Hebrew Bible. They rejected the oral tradition and the interpretations of the Pharisees, which was passed down from generation to generation and was seen as an oral supplement to the written law. They also rejected the idea of the resurrection of the dead, and the belief in angels and spirits.

Role in Jewish Politics

The Sadducees were a powerful and influential group in Jewish politics during the Second Temple period. They had close ties to the ruling powers of the time, including the Hasmonean dynasty and the Roman Empire. They held positions of power within the Jewish government, including the position of the High Priest, which gave them significant influence in religious and political matters.

Their political power and influence allowed them to suppress the other Jewish sects, such as the Pharisees, which they saw as a threat to their religious and political authority. They also used their power to suppress popular movements that challenged their authority, such as the Zealot movement, which advocated for Jewish independence and resistance against Roman rule.

Relationship with the Pharisees

The Sadducees had a strained relationship with the Pharisees, another Jewish sect that emerged in the Second Temple period. The Sadducees rejected the oral tradition and the interpretations of the Pharisees, which was passed down from generation to generation and was seen as an oral supplement to the written law. The Pharisees, on the other hand, believed in the oral tradition and the interpretations, and saw the Sadducees as a threat to their religious authority.

This disagreement led to a rivalry between the two sects, with the Sadducees using their political power to suppress the Pharisees and their beliefs. This rivalry also contributed to the division among the Jewish people during the Second Temple period.

Decline

The Sadducees' power and influence began to decline after the Roman Empire destroyed the Second Temple in 70 CE. With the destruction of the Temple, the Sadducees lost their main source of power and authority, as they were the chief priests and temple officials. The loss of the temple also meant the end of the sacrifices, which were the heart of their religious practices. Additionally, the rise of Christianity, which rejected the Sadducees' beliefs in the resurrection of the dead, further contributed to the decline of the Sadducees.

In conclusion, the Sadducees were a Jewish sect that emerged in the Second Temple period. They were a powerful and influential group of religious leaders, who were primarily made up of the upper class and the aristocracy of Jewish society. They held positions of power within the Jewish government, including the position of the High Priest, which gave them significant influence in religious and political matters. They rejected the oral tradition and the interpretations of the Pharisees and rejected the idea of the resurrection of the dead, and the belief in angels and spirits. The Sadducees' power and influence began to decline after the Roman Empire destroyed the Second Temple in 70 CE. With the destruction of the Temple, the Sadducees lost their main source of power and authority, as they were the chief priests and temple officials. The loss of the temple also meant the end of the sacrifices, which were the heart of their religious practices. Additionally, the rise of Christianity, which rejected the Sadducees' beliefs in the resurrection of the dead, further contributed to the decline of the Sadducees.

After the fall of the Second Temple and the end of the Sadducee religious practices, they faded away as a sect and their influence on Jewish religious and political life came to an end. It is important to note that the Sadducees, along with the Pharisees, Essenes and other sects, were part of a diverse Jewish society during the Second Temple period, and their beliefs and practices contributed to the rich tapestry of Jewish thought and tradition.

In conclusion, the Sadducees were a powerful and influential Jewish sect that played a significant role in Jewish politics and religion during the Second Temple period. They had distinct beliefs and practices that set them apart from other Jewish sects, but their decline after the fall of the Second Temple marked the end of their religious and political influence.

CHAPTER 24 Pharisees, Jewish Religious Leaders

The Pharisees were a Jewish sect that emerged in the Second Temple period. They were a powerful and influential group of religious leaders who played a significant role in Jewish politics and religion during the Second Temple period.

Background

The Pharisees were a Jewish sect that emerged in the Second Temple period, which lasted from 516 BC to 70 CE. They were a powerful and influential group of religious leaders, who believed in the interpretation and application of the written Torah, which consists of the first five books of the Hebrew Bible. They also believed in the oral tradition, which was passed down from generation to generation and was seen as an oral supplement to the written law.

Beliefs

The Pharisees believed in the interpretation and application of the written Torah, which consists of the first five books of the Hebrew Bible. They also believed in the oral tradition, which was passed down from generation to generation and was seen as an oral supplement to the written law. They also believed in the resurrection of the dead, the existence of angels and spirits, and the coming of a Messiah. They were known for their emphasis on personal piety and religious observance, which were considered essential for salvation.

Role in Jewish Politics

The Pharisees were a powerful and influential group in Jewish politics during the Second Temple period. They were a popular movement among the common people, and had a significant following among the Jewish population. They were known for their emphasis on personal piety and religious observance, which were considered essential for salvation. They had close ties to the ruling powers of the time, including the Hasmonean dynasty and the Roman Empire, and they held positions of power within the Jewish government, including the position of the High Priest, which gave them significant influence in religious and political matters.

Relationship with the Sadducees

The Pharisees had a strained relationship with the Sadducees, another Jewish sect that emerged in the Second Temple period. The Sadducees rejected the oral tradition and the interpretations of the Pharisees, which the Pharisees considered as an oral supplement to the written law. The Pharisees, on the other hand, believed in the oral tradition and the interpretations, and saw the Sadducees as a threat to their religious authority.

This disagreement led to a rivalry between the two sects, with the Sadducees using their political power to suppress the Pharisees and their beliefs. The Pharisees, however, had a significant following among the common people and they were able to preserve their beliefs and practices. This rivalry also contributed to the division among the Jewish people during the Second Temple period.

Influence on Jewish Thought and Practice

The Pharisees had a significant influence on Jewish thought and practice during the Second Temple period and beyond. They emphasized the importance of personal piety and religious observance, which were considered essential for salvation. They also contributed to the development of the Mishnah, the first written collection of Jewish oral law, which was later developed into the Talmud.

The Pharisees' emphasis on personal piety and religious observance had a lasting impact on Jewish thought and practice. Their ideas and beliefs were passed down through the generations and continue to influence Jewish religious practice to this day.

Decline and Legacy

The Pharisees' power and influence began to decline after the Roman Empire destroyed the Second Temple in 70 CE. With the destruction of the Temple, the Pharisees lost their main source of power and authority, as they were the chief priests and temple officials. However, their beliefs, practices, and teachings were preserved in the Mishnah and Talmud, which continued to shape Jewish thought and practice.

The legacy of the Pharisees can be seen in the modern-day Jewish religious practices and beliefs. The Pharisees' emphasis on personal piety and religious observance, along with their contributions to the Mishnah and Talmud, continue to shape Jewish religious thought and practice.

In conclusion, the Pharisees were a powerful and influential Jewish sect that played a significant role in Jewish politics and religion during the Second Temple period. They had distinct beliefs and practices that set them apart from other Jewish sects, and they had a significant following among the Jewish population. They believed in the interpretation and application of the written Torah, oral tradition, the resurrection of the dead, the existence of angels and spirits, and the coming of a Messiah. Their influence on Jewish thought and practice is still felt today, and their ideas and beliefs continue to shape Jewish religious practice.

Edward D. Andrews

CHAPTER 25 Herod the Great

Image 35 Herod's Temple as depicted on the Holyland Model of Jerusalem. The expansion of the Temple was Herod's most ambitious project.

Image 36 Copper coin of Herod, bearing the legend "ΒΑΣΙΛΕΩΣ ΗΡΩΔΟΥ" ("Basileōs Hērōdou") on the obverse

The Herod family were a group of political leaders who ruled over the Jewish people. They were originally from the Idumean tribe, also known as Edomites, but had been forcibly converted to Judaism by the Maccabean ruler John Hyrcanus I in around 125 BC. Most of what is known about the Herods comes from the historical writings of Josephus. The family's patriarch was Antipater I, who was appointed governor of Idumea by the Hasmonaean king Alexander Jannaeus. Antipater I's son, also named Antipater or Antipas, was the father of Herod the Great. Despite claims by the historian Nicholas of Damascus that Antipater II was of Jewish descent, Josephus asserts that this was merely to appease Herod, who was actually of Edomite heritage on both his mother and father's side. Antipater II was a wealthy and ambitious man who supported John Hyrcanus II in his bid for the position of Jewish high priest and king. However, Antipater II ultimately had his own agenda and was granted Roman citizenship and the governorship of Judea by Julius Caesar. He appointed his sons Phasael and Herod as governors of Jerusalem and Galilee respectively. However, his career came to an end when he was assassinated by poisoning.

Herod the Great

Herod the Great was the second son of Antipater II and his wife Cypros. He is often portrayed in history as a ruthless, cunning, and immoral individual, with a reputation for being suspicious, cruel, and even murderous. However, he also possessed his father's diplomatic abilities and opportunistic nature. Additionally, he was a skilled organizer and military commander, as described by Josephus as a man of great physical strength and proficient in horseback riding, as well as using weapons such as javelins and bows. He is also known for his building prowess and was able to improve his reputation as governor of Galilee by eliminating local bandit groups. However, some members of the Jewish community were envious of his success and, along with the mothers of the slain bandits, convinced Hyrcanus II, the high priest, to summon Herod before the Sanhedrin for executing the robbers without proper trial. Despite being subject to the court as a proselyte, Herod appeared before them with a bodyguard, which further angered the judges. One judge, Samaias (Simeon), even predicted that if Herod escaped punishment, he would eventually kill the judges themselves. However, Hyrcanus II was a weak-willed leader and, under pressure from Herod's intimidation and a letter from Sextus Caesar, the president of Syria, the charges were dismissed

King of Judea

Herod, also known as Herod the Great, was a king of Judea who came to power after his father's death. In 39 BC, he was appointed king of greater Judea by the Roman senate, however, it took him three years to establish himself as the de facto king when he captured Jerusalem and deposed Antigonus, the son of Aristobulus. In order to maintain his position, Herod took extreme measures such as convincing the Roman leader Mark Antony to kill Antigonus and executing 45 members of Antigonus' party. He even killed John Hyrcanus II, a high priest and political leader, years later. He was a skilled politician and believed that his best interests lay in supporting Rome, frequently changing sides to align with the shifting fortunes of the Roman leaders. He was able to maintain the friendship of Augustus Caesar, the first Roman emperor, by means of large bribes and smooth speech. He was able to win out when complaints or charges were brought against him to Rome, sometimes by members of his own household. He first served as governor of Galilee, then as governor of Coele-Syria under Cassius, and eventually as king of Judea at the recommendation of Mark Antony. Augustus Caesar later added the regions of Samaria, Gadara, Gaza, Joppa, Trachonitis, Batanaea, Auranitis, Perea, and Idumea to his kingdom, an area east of the Jordan roughly corresponding to Gilead.

Temple and Other Building Works

Herod the Great was known for his extensive building projects, the most notable of which was the rebuilding of the temple of Zerubbabel in Jerusalem. The temple, which was constructed at great cost and described as magnificent by Josephus, took 18 months to build according to his account, but was stated by the Jews to have taken 46 years, as mentioned in a conversation with Jesus Christ. Other structures he built included theaters, amphitheaters, hippodromes, citadels, fortresses, palaces, gardens, temples in honor of Caesar, aqueducts, monuments, and even cities, many of which were named after himself, his relatives, or the emperors of Rome. He also built an artificial harbor at Caesarea that rivaled the seaport of Tyre, and reconstructed the fortresses of Antonia and Masada, making the latter particularly magnificent. His building achievements were not limited to Jerusalem but spread to cities as far as Antioch in Syria and Rhodes. However, despite his building achievements, many of the Jewish people resented him for his lavish entertainment and free gifts to

Roman dignitaries, as well as for building amphitheaters and promoting pagan festivities. He even went as far as participating in the Olympic Games in Greece and donating money to perpetuate them. Despite being nominally a Jew, Herod's actions and lifestyle were seen as a complete denial of his claim to be a servant of Jehovah God.

Trouble in Family

The Herod family was known for their ambition, suspicion, immorality, and troubling behavior. However, Herod the Great faced the majority of his difficulties and sorrows within his own family. His mother Cypros and his sister Salome were a constant source of aggravation. Herod was married to Mariamne, the granddaughter of Hyrcanus II and daughter of Alexander, who was the son of Aristobulus. Though Mariamne was a beautiful woman, and Herod deeply loved her, his mother and sister developed a deep hatred for her. This led to Herod's constant suspicion that members of his family, particularly his sons, were plotting against him. In some cases, his suspicions were justified. His greed for power and constant suspicion led him to order the murder of his wife Mariamne, three of his sons, his wife's brother and grandfather (Hyrcanus), several of his closest friends, and many others. He even went as far as using torture to extract confessions from those he suspected had information that would confirm his suspicions.

Relationship With the Jews

Herod the Great's relationship with the Jewish people was complicated. On one hand, he attempted to gain their favor by rebuilding the temple in Jerusalem and providing necessities during times of famine. He also lowered taxes for some of his subjects and even obtained privileges for Jews in various parts of the world from Augustus Caesar. However, his tyrannical and cruel behavior outweighed these efforts, and he faced constant trouble with the Jewish people throughout most of his rule. Despite his attempts to appease the Jews, his actions were not enough to reconcile his tyrannical rule and cruelty.

Prosperity

During the period of 25-14 BC, King Herod's reign was marked by prosperity and splendor. In terms of cultural developments, he introduced the quinquennial games in honor of Caesar, built theaters, amphitheaters, and hippodromes. He also constructed many fortresses and temples in gentile territories. One of his greatest achievements was the rebuilding of the temple in Jerusalem, which was begun in 20 BC and completed in 63 A.D. He also familiarized himself with Greek culture by surrounding himself with men of Hellenistic education. In terms of domestic changes, he married Mariamne II, daughter of Simon and appointed him as high priest. He also sent his two sons to Rome for their education, and upon their return, they married into powerful families. In terms of political advances, Augustus awarded him new territories and made the procurators of Syria responsible to him. To show appreciation, he built a beautiful temple for Augustus in Zenodorus's territory. However, to pacify the people who were resentful of his emphasis on Greco-Roman culture and religion, he remitted a third of the people's taxes, forbade them to congregate and ordered them to take a loyalty oath.

Domestic Troubles

The last decade of King Herod's life was marked by political intrigue and infighting among his sons. This was due to the fact that he had ten wives, each of whom wanted her son(s) to be his successor. Herod had several children, but his two favorite sons were Alexander and Aristobulus, who were the sons of his first wife Mariamne I. When they returned from their education in Rome in 17 or 16 BC, new domestic troubles arose. His sister Salome, who had an intense hatred towards these two sons, wanted her own son to succeed to the throne. Salome and Pheroras (brother of Herod and Salome) warned Herod that these two sons were out to avenge their mother's murder by bringing charges against him before Caesar that would cause him to lose his throne. This situation was further complicated by the fact that Alexander and Aristobulus were Hasmoneans, and at times they were arrogant, which led to Salome speaking ill of their mother whom Herod had killed.

In 14 BC, King Herod became disturbed by the reckless behavior of his favorite sons, Alexander and Aristobulus. As a result, he recalled his oldest son Antipater (son of Doris) from exile in order to curb their behavior. In 13 BC, Herod made a new will, in which he made Antipater the sole heir of his domain. He sent Antipater and his friend Agrippa to present the will to the emperor Augustus in the hopes that it would be ratified. However, Antipater realized that Herod could change his mind again and from Rome, he wrote slanderous letters against Alexander and Aristobulus to Herod. This further infuriated Herod and in 12 BC, he brought Alexander and Aristobulus before Augustus in Aquileia (near Venice) to be tried. However, the case resulted in reconciliation rather than execution. Returning home with Alexander, Aristobulus, and Antipater, Herod made a third will naming all three sons as his successors. The situation was complex and uncertain and it was driven by the personal ambition of the sons and their mother's desire to see their own son as the successor.

After returning from Rome around 11 or 10 BC, Antipater, with the help of Herod's sister Salome and brother Pheroras, began to once again slander Alexander and Aristobulus, which again aroused Herod's suspicions. Antipater furnished proof from one of Alexander's friends that Alexander, with the help of Aristobulus, was planning to kill Herod and flee to Rome to lay claim on Herod's kingdom. As a result, Herod imprisoned Alexander. However, Alexander's father-in-law, the king of Cappadocia, Archelaus, was concerned about the welfare of his own daughter, and was able to reconcile Herod and Alexander. This brought peace again to Herod's household.

However, Herod still had some difficulties with external enemies and even with the emperor Augustus. About forty of Herod's subjects in Trachonitis had become rebellious and fled to a neighboring Arab territory under the ruler Syllaeus, who had overthrown the king Obodas. In consultation with Saturninus and Volumnius, governors of Syria, Herod entered the Arab territory to capture the rebels, and killed 25 Arabs who had come in defense of the rebels. Syllaeus, however, went before Augustus in Rome to accuse Herod of devastating the

Arab territory and killing 25,000 Arabs. Augustus believed Syllaeus, and wrote to Herod that he was to be treated as a subject and no longer a "friend of Caesar", a most coveted title. Herod immediately sent an embassy to Rome to defend himself, and when this failed, he sent a second under the leadership of Nicolas of Damascus.

While awaiting the emperor's decision, new domestic issues arose in Herod's household. A man named Eurycles from Lacedemon, acting on behalf of Antipater, played Alexander and Aristobulus against Herod. Other troublemakers became involved, and Herod became increasingly suspicious of his sons. He imprisoned Alexander and Aristobulus and accused them of plotting against him in a report to the emperor Augustus.

Meanwhile, Nicolas of Damascus had an audience with Augustus in Rome and explained the true situation concerning Herod and the Arabs. When Augustus fully understood the situation, he executed Syllaeus and reconciled with Herod. At the same time, messengers from Herod arrived in Rome seeking the emperor's advice regarding his sons. Augustus gave Herod full authority to deal with his sons as he wished but advised him to have a trial outside of Herod's territory at Berytus (Beirut) with Roman officials attending it. In accordance with the emperor's advice, there was a trial in Berytus and the court pronounced the death sentence upon Alexander and Aristobulus. Thus, at Sebaste (Samaria), where Herod had married Mariamne thirty years before, her two sons were executed by strangulation, probably in 7 BC. This wiped out the Hasmonean line, with the exception of Herodias, Antipas's wife, and her brother Agrippa I, who began his rule in AD 37.

Herod now made his fourth will, naming Antipater as the sole successor to his kingdom. However, Antipater was impatient and began secretly conferring with Herod's brother Pheroras, the tetrarch of Perea. Salome, Herod's sister, became aware of these conferences and reported their intention to kill Herod to him. This caused a significant strain in Herod's relationship with Antipater. Realizing this, Antipater arranged for Augustus to request that Herod send him to Rome. Herod sent Antipater to Rome with the new will that named him as the sole ruler, and in the event that Antipater's death occurred before his own, he named Herod (Philip), son of Mariamne II, as his successor.

While Antipater was in Rome, Pheroras died. Upon investigation, Herod found that Pheroras had been killed by poison sent by Antipater, which had been intended for Herod himself. From the female slaves of Pheroras, Herod learned of Antipater's meetings with Pheroras, his complaints about Herod's long life, and the uncertainties of his own prospects for the throne. Herod recalled Antipater from Rome under false pretenses, and upon his return, immediately imprisoned him in the king's palace. The next day, he was tried before Varus, the governor of Syria, and was without defense. Herod put him in chains and sent a report to Augustus. Meanwhile, another plot of Antipater against Herod was unveiled. Becoming very ill and realizing that his death was near, Herod drew up his fifth will, wherein he omitted Antipater and his next two oldest sons, Archelaus and Philip, because Antipater had poisoned his mind against them. He selected his youngest son Antipas, son of the Samaritan Malthace, as his sole successor.

In the winter of 2 1 B.C, it is believed that Jesus was born. Magi, also known as wise men, traveled to Jerusalem to inquire about the birthplace of the newborn king of the Jews. King Herod, who was in power at the time, summoned the magi to ask them for the exact location of the Christ child so that he could also go and worship him. However, when the wise men found Jesus in Bethlehem, they were warned in a dream to return home another way. Additionally, the Lord appeared to Joseph in a dream and instructed him to flee to Egypt due to Herod's desire to kill the child. As a result of this, Herod killed all the male children in Bethlehem who were two years old or younger.

As Herod grew older, he became increasingly ill, and his health continued to deteriorate. Two rabbis, Judas son of Sepphoraeus, and Matthias son of Margalus, incited the people to tear down an eagle symbol from the temple gate, believing it would be pleasing to God. Despite his weak condition, Herod punished the offenders by ordering them to be burned alive.

When Herod realized that the warm spring baths at Callirrhoe were no longer helping his diseases, he returned to Jericho. He ordered notable Jews from all parts of the nation to come to him, and when they arrived, he locked them in the hippodrome. Knowing that the people disliked him, he ordered his sister Salome and her husband Alexas to slay all the leaders in the hippodrome at the moment of his death, in order to ensure national mourning rather than a festival.

At this time, Herod received a letter from Rome in which the emperor granted him permission to execute his son Antipater, which he did immediately. In his final will, Herod selected Archelaus, the older son of Malthace, as king, his brother Antipas as tetrarch of Galilee and Perea, and their half-brother Philip as tetrarch of Gaulanitis, Trachonitis, Batanea, and Paneas.

His Sickness and Death

Herod's death was a result of a loathsome disease, accompanied by fever and intense itching, continuous pain in the intestines, tumors in the feet, inflammation of the abdomen and gangrene of the privy parts, engendering worms, in addition to asthma, difficulty in breathing, and convulsions in all his limbs. This was likely due to his licentious living. During his fatal sickness, he ordered the murder of his scheming son Antipater, knowing that the Jews would rejoice upon hearing of his own death. He commanded the most illustrious men of the Jewish nation to gather at a place called the Hippodrome, at Jericho, and had them shut in. He then gave a command to those near him that, when he died, the news of his death should not be announced until these Jewish leaders were first killed, so that every family in Judea would certainly weep at his funeral. However, this order was never carried out as his sister Salome and her husband Alexas freed these men and sent them to their homes. Herod died at the age of around 70 years and had made a will designating his son Antipas as his successor. But shortly before his death, he added a codicil or made a new will appointing Archelaus to that position. Archelaus was acknowledged by the people and the army as king, but the action was contested by Antipas. After a hearing of the matter in Rome, Augustus Caesar upheld Archelaus, but he constituted Archelaus an ethnarch and divided the territory formerly ruled over by Herod: half went to Archelaus; Antipas and Philip, two of Herod's other sons, were granted a share each in the other half.

Slaughter of Children

The Bible account of the slaughter of all the boys two years of age and under in Bethlehem and its districts, carried out by King Herod, is in line with other historical accounts that describe his cruel and ruthless nature. This event took place shortly before Herod's death. As a result of this, Jesus and his parents had to flee to Egypt, but they returned and settled in Galilee after Herod's death. These two events, the slaughter of the children and the escape of Jesus, were foretold by Jehovah through his prophets Jeremiah and Hosea. This event is described in the Bible in the book of Matthew chapter 2:1-23, as well as in the book of Jeremiah chapter 31:15 and the book of Hosea chapter 11:1.

Date of His Death

The exact date of King Herod's death is a matter of debate among historians. Some believe that he died in the year 5 or 4 BC, basing their chronology largely on the historical accounts of Josephus. However, there are inconsistencies in Josephus' dating methods that lead to confusion about the actual year of Herod's death.

Josephus uses a "consular dating" method, which is based on the rule of certain Roman consuls, to date the time that Herod was appointed king by Rome. According to this method, Herod's appointment as king would be in 40 BC, but another historian, Appianos, places the event in 39 BC. Josephus also places Herod's capture of Jerusalem in 37 BC, but he also states that this occurred 27 years after the capture of the city by Pompey (in 63 BC). This would make the date of Herod's taking of the city of Jerusalem 36 BC.

Josephus also states that Herod died 37 years from the time that he was appointed king by the Romans, and 34 years after he took Jerusalem. However, these years may be counted in a different way in

Jewish tradition, using the "accession-year method" which was used for the kings of the line of David. This method could mean that Herod's death could have been in 1 BC.

Additionally, Josephus states that Herod died not long after an eclipse of the moon and before a Passover. Since there was an eclipse on March 11, 4 BC (March 13, Julian), some historians have concluded that this was the eclipse referred to by Josephus.

Another line of evidence that supports that King Herod died in 1 BC is the occurrence of eclipses. There was a total eclipse of the moon in 1 BC., about three months before Passover, while the one in 4 BC. was only partial. The total eclipse in 1 BC was on January 8 (January 10, Julian), 18 days before Shebat 2, the traditional day of Herod's death. Another eclipse (partial) occurred on December 27 of 1 BC (December 29, Julian).

Another line of evidence is based on the age of Herod at the time of his death. According to Josephus, he was about 70 years old. Josephus states that when Herod received his appointment as governor of Galilee, which is generally dated 47 BC, he was 15 years old. However, scholars have understood this to be an error and that 25 years were intended. This would indicate that Herod's death occurred in 2 or 1 BC. However, it should be noted that Josephus has many inconsistencies in his dating of events and is therefore not a reliable source.

The Bible provides the most reliable evidence on the date of Herod's death. The historian Luke in the Bible tells us that John came baptizing in the 15th year of Tiberius Caesar. By counting back 30 years from this point, it brings us to the fall of 2 BC as the time of the human birth of Jesus Christ. This aligns with the prophecy of the "seventy weeks" in the book of Daniel. Therefore, the available evidence suggests that King Herod likely died in the year 1 BC.

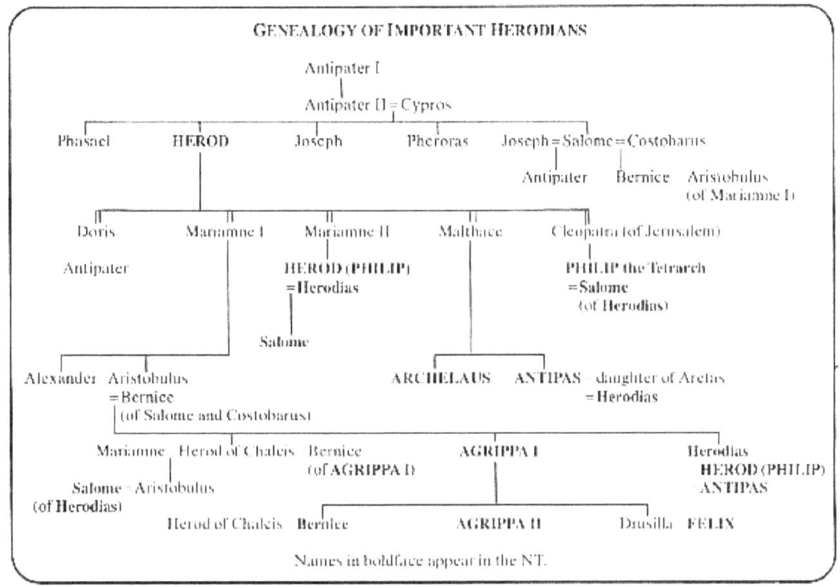

The Astrologers Who Visited Jesus

The Bible account in Matthew tells us that after Jesus was born in Bethlehem, astrologers from eastern parts came to Jerusalem saying that they saw his star when they were in the east. King Herod, suspicious of this news, questioned the chief priests and scribes about the location of the Christ's birth and then asked the astrologers for the time of the star's appearance. This event happened sometime after Jesus' birth, as he was now not in the manger but with his parents in a house. When the astrologers failed to return to Herod with the whereabouts of the young child, the king ordered the slaughter of all boys two years of age and under throughout Bethlehem and its districts. Jesus and his parents fled to Egypt as a result of God's warning.

The timing of this event can be inferred from the fact that the death of King Herod could hardly have taken place before 1 BC. If that were the case, Jesus, born around October 1, 2 BC, would have been less than three months old. Additionally, it is not necessary for Jesus to have been two years old when the killing of the children occurred, he could have been less than a year old, as Herod calculated from the time the star appeared to the astrologers. This journey could have taken months, as astrologers likely came from Babylon or Mesopotamia, which was a long journey.

In summary, the Bible chronology, astronomical data, and available historical records seem to indicate that the time of King Herod's death was in 1 BC or possibly early in 1 AD.

APPENDIX A Apocryphal Works

First Maccabees is a historical account of the Jewish struggle for independence during the second century BC. It covers the period from the beginning of Antiochus Epiphanes' reign in 175 BC to the death of Simon Maccabaeus in around 134 BC. The book is particularly focused on the exploits of the priest Mattathias and his sons, Judas, Jonathan, and Simon, in their battles with the Syrians. "First Maccabees" is considered to be the most valuable of the Apocryphal works because of the historical information it provides for this period. However, it should be noted that the book presents history from a human perspective, meaning that it may not be entirely accurate. The Jewish Encyclopedia (1976, Vol. VIII, p. 243) comments that "history is written from the human standpoint." Like the other Apocryphal works, it did not form part of the inspired Hebrew canon, it was evidently written in Hebrew about the latter part of the second century BC. The book of First Maccabees is considered to be a non-canonical text and is not considered to be a part of the official canon of the Bible by most Christian denominations.

Second Maccabees is a historical account that covers part of the same time period as "First Maccabees" (around 180 BC to 160 BC), but it was not written by the same author. The writer of "Second Maccabees" presents the book as a summary of the previous works of a certain Jason of Cyrene. It describes the persecutions of the Jews under Antiochus Epiphanes, the plundering of the Temple, and its subsequent rededication. The account also includes a depiction of Jeremiah as carrying the tabernacle and the Ark of the Covenant to a cave in the mountain from which Moses viewed the land of Canaan, which contradicts historical fact. The book also includes various texts used in Catholic dogma as support for doctrines such as punishment after death, intercession by the saints and the propriety of prayers for the dead. The style of the book is described as "hellenistic" and not of the best quality, being at times turgid and frequently pompous. The writer of Second Maccabees makes no claim of writing under divine inspiration, and in fact, devotes part of the second chapter to justify his choice of the particular method used in handling the subject material. The book was evidently written in Greek, sometime between 134 BC and the fall of Jerusalem in 70 CE. Like the other Apocryphal works, it did not form part of the inspired Hebrew canon and is considered to be a non-canonical text and is not considered to be a part of the official canon of the Bible by most Christian denominations.

Apocryphal Books

The term "apocryphal" is derived from the Greek word "apokryphos," which originally referred to things that were "carefully concealed." When applied to writings, it originally meant texts that were not read publicly, or "concealed" from others. However, over time, the meaning of the term shifted to imply texts that were spurious or not considered part of the canon. In present-day usage, the term is most commonly applied to the collection of texts that were declared as part of the Bible canon by the Roman Catholic Church at the Council of Trent in 1546. These texts, which include Tobit, Judith, Wisdom, Sirach (Ecclesiasticus), Baruch, and 1 and 2 Maccabees, are referred to by Catholic writers as deuterocanonical, meaning "of the second (or later) canon," as distinguished from the texts that are considered part of the canon, known as protocanonical. These texts provide important historical and cultural context for the religious beliefs and practices of Jewish people during the intertestamental period, as well as insight into the political and social conditions of the time. They also offer a deeper understanding of the historical context of the New Testament.

Evidence Against Canonicity

The canonicity of the Apocryphal or Deuterocanonical books is highly debated among scholars. While they do have certain historical value, there is no solid foundation for considering them as part of the canon of inspired Scriptures. The evidence suggests that the canon of Hebrew Scriptures was closed following the writing of Ezra, Nehemiah, and Malachi in the 5th century BC. These texts were never included in the Jewish canon and are not considered part of it today.

This is supported by the testimony of the first-century Jewish historian Josephus, who stated that the Jewish people only recognized a limited number of books as sacred and that these were distinct from the Apocryphal writings. He wrote that "We do not possess myriads of inconsistent books, conflicting with each other. Our books, those which are justly accredited, are but two and twenty [equivalent to the 39 books of the Hebrew Scriptures according to modern division], and contain the record of all time." He further acknowledged the existence of the Apocryphal books and their exclusion from the canon by adding, "From Artaxerxes to our own time the complete history has been written but has not been deemed worthy of equal credit with the earlier records, because of the failure of the exact succession of the prophets." Overall, while the Apocryphal books offer historical and cultural context, evidence suggests that they were not considered as part of the canon of inspired scripture by ancient Jewish communities

Inclusion in Greek Septuagint

Arguments in favor of the canonicity of the Apocryphal or Deuterocanonical books often center around the fact that these texts are included in many early copies of the Greek Septuagint translation of the Hebrew Scriptures, which began around 280 BC. However, since no original copies of the Septuagint are extant, it cannot be definitively stated that these texts were originally included in that translation. Many, if not most, of the Apocryphal writings were written after the Septuagint translation was started, and therefore were not part of the original list of books selected for translation by the translators. At best, they can be considered as later additions to the Septuagint. Furthermore, while the Greek-speaking Jews of Alexandria eventually included these texts in their Septuagint translations and viewed them as part of an expanded canon of sacred writings, it is clear that they were never accepted into the Jerusalem or Palestinian canon. They were viewed as secondary writings and not of divine origin. This is reinforced by the decision of the Jewish Council of Jamnia around 90 CE, which specifically excluded all such writings from the Hebrew canon. The importance of considering the Jewish perspective on this matter is highlighted by the Apostle Paul in Romans 3:1-2.

Additional Ancient Testimony

One of the key arguments against the canonicity of the Apocryphal or Deuterocanonical books is the fact that none of the Christian Bible writers quoted from these texts. While this alone is not conclusive, as there are also a few books recognized as canonical that are not quoted by these writers, such as Esther, Ecclesiastes, and The Song of Solomon, the fact that not one of the Apocryphal writings is quoted even once is certainly noteworthy. Additionally, leading Bible scholars and "church fathers" of the first centuries of the Common Era generally gave the Apocryphal books an inferior position. For example, Origen, a prominent Christian scholar of the early 3rd century CE, made a distinction between these texts and those of the true canon. Similarly, Athanasius, Cyril of Jerusalem, Gregory of Nazianzus, and Amphilocius, all of the 4th century CE, prepared catalogs of sacred writings in accordance with the Hebrew canon and either ignored these additional writings or placed them in a secondary class. Jerome, who is considered "the best Hebrew scholar" of the early church and who completed the Latin Vulgate in 405 CE, explicitly rejected these Apocryphal books and was the first to use the word "Apocrypha" in the sense of non-canonical in reference to these texts. In his prologue to the books of Samuel and Kings, Jerome listed the inspired books of the Hebrew Scriptures in accordance with the Hebrew canon and stated that "whatever is beyond these must be put in the apocrypha." He advised that these texts be read with caution, and that one should be aware that they are not truly written by the authors to whom they are attributed and that they contain many inaccuracies.

Differing Catholic Views

The trend towards including the Apocryphal or Deuterocanonical books as canonical was primarily initiated by Augustine, a prominent Christian theologian of the 4th century CE. However, even Augustine acknowledged in his later works that there was a clear distinction between the books of the Hebrew canon and these "outside books." The Catholic Church, following Augustine's lead, included these additional writings in the canon of sacred books determined by the Council of Carthage in 397 CE. However, it wasn't until the Council of Trent in 1546 CE that the Roman Catholic Church officially confirmed its acceptance of these books as part of its canon of Bible books, due to the fact that even within the church, opinion was still divided over these writings. John Wycliffe, a Catholic priest and scholar who in the 14th century made the first translation of the Bible into English, included the Apocrypha in his work, but in the preface to this translation declared such writings to be "without authority of belief." Similarly, Dominican Cardinal Cajetan, a prominent Catholic theologian of his time (1469-1534 CE) also differentiated between the books of the true Hebrew canon and the Apocryphal works, citing Jerome as an authority. It is important to note that the Council of Trent did not accept all the writings previously approved by the earlier Council of Carthage, it dropped three of these: the Prayer of Manasses and 1 and 2 Esdras (not the 1 and 2 Esdras that in the Catholic Douay Bible correspond with Ezra and Nehemiah). These three writings, which had appeared in the approved Latin Vulgate for over 1,100 years, were now excluded.

Internal Evidence

The internal evidence of the Apocryphal or Deuterocanonical books also supports the argument against their canonicity. These texts lack the prophetic element present in the canonical books. Their teachings and contents, at times, contradict those of the canon, and they also contain contradictions within themselves. They are filled with historical and geographic inaccuracies and anachronisms. The writers of some of these texts are even guilty of dishonesty by falsely representing their works as those of earlier, inspired writers. Additionally, these texts display evidence of influence from pagan Greek ideas, and at times employ an extravagant language and literary style that is foreign to the inspired Scriptures. Two of the writers even imply that they were not inspired (as seen in the Prologue to Ecclesiasticus; 2 Maccabees 2:24-32; 15:38-40). Therefore, it can be said that the best evidence against the canonicity of the Apocrypha is the Apocrypha itself. Further examination of individual books within the Apocrypha will provide further insight.

Bibliography

Atkinson, K. (2016). *A History of the Hasmonean State: Josephus and Beyond.* London, UK: Bloomsbury Publishing.

Bar-Kochva, B. (1989). *Judas Maccabaeus: The Jewish Struggle Against the Seleucids.* Cambridge, England: Cambridge University Press.

Brand, C., Draper, C., & Archie, E. (2003). *Holman Illustrated Bible Dictionary: Revised, Updated and Expanded.* Nashville, TN: Holman.

Bromiley, G. W. (1986). *The International Standard Bible Encyclopedia (Vol. 1-4).* Grand Rapids, MI: William B. Eerdmans Publishing Co.

Cohen, S. J. (2006). *From the Maccabees to the Mishnah (Second Edition).* Louisville, KY: Westminster John Knox Press.

Doran, R., & Attridge, H. W. (2012). *2 Maccabees: A Critical Commentary. Hermeneia.:* . Minneapolis, MN: Augsburg Fortress Press.

Elwell, W. A., & Beitzel, B. J. (1988). *Baker Encyclopedia of the Bible.* Grand Rapids, MI: Baker Book House.

Feldman, L. H., & Reinhold, M. (1996). *Jewish Life and Thought Among Greeks and Romans.* Minneapolis, MN: Fortress Press.

Fortier, E. H. (1988). *Judas Maccabeus.* New York City, NY: Chelsea House Publishers.

Grainger, J. D. (2012). *The Wars of the Maccabees.* Havertown, PA: Casemate Publishers.

Harrington, D. J. (2009). *The Maccabean Revolt: Anatomy of a Biblical Revolution. :* . Eugene, Oregon: Wipf and Stock.

Johnston, S. I. (2004). *Religions of the Ancient World: A Guide.* Cambridge, MA: Harvard University Press.

Josephus, F., & Whiston, W. (1987). *The Works of Josephus: Complete and Unabridged.* Peabody, MA: Hendrickson.

Myers, A. C. (1987). *The Eerdmans Bible Dictionary* . Grand Rapids, Mich: Eerdmans.

Noam, V., & Translated by Ordan, D. (2018). *Shifting Images of the Hasmoneans: Second Temple Legends and Their Reception in Josephus and Rabbinic literature.* Oxford, England: Oxford University Press.

Oesterley, W. (1939). *A History of Israel.* Oxford, England: Clarendon Press.

Scott Jr., J. J. (1995). *Jewish Backgrounds of the New Testament* . Grand Rapids, MI: Baker Publishing Group.

Wood, D. R. (1996). *New Bible Dictionary (Third Edition).* Downers Grove: InterVarsity Press.

Wood, L. J. (1986). *A Survey of Israel's History.* . Grand Rapids, MI: Zondervan.